BEST PRACTICES IN CONSTRUCTION SITE SAFETY

WHERE WE HAVE BEEN, WHERE WE ARE GOING, AND A REVIEW OF CONSTRUCTION THROUGH THE YEARS

Harlan Fair

**Best Practices in Construction Site Safety:
Where We have Been, Where We are Going,
and a Review of Construction Through the Years**

Copyright © 2020 Harlan Fair.

Produced and printed
by Stillwater River Publications.
All rights reserved. Written and produced in the
United States of America. This book may not be reproduced
or sold in any form without the expressed, written
permission of the author and publisher.

Visit our website at
www.StillwaterPress.com
for more information.

First Stillwater River Publications Edition

ISBN: 978-1-952521-22-5

1 2 3 4 5 6 7 8 9 10
Written by Harlan Fair
Published by Stillwater River Publications,
Pawtucket, RI, USA.

*The views and opinions expressed
in this book are solely those of the author
and do not necessarily reflect the views
and opinions of the publisher.*

TABLE OF CONTENTS

Preface .... *i*

Part I: Sixty-Eight Years of Experience and Observation
    Chapter 1: Construction History 1
    Chapter 2: Forensic / Legal Aspects 7
    Chapter 3: Specifics to Crane Safety Development 20
    Chapter 4: Experience 22

Part II: Manual of Best Practice in Construction
    Chapter 5: Construction Delivery Systems 33
    Chapter 6: Construction Site Safety 38
    Chapter 7: Crane Safety 44
    Chapter 8: Regulations and Standards 63

Part III: Where We Are Going
    Chapter 9: Diversity In Construction 75
    Chapter 10: Prevention Through Design 76
    Chapter 11: The New Technology: AI and the Digitized World 78

Index 87

PREFACE

This book is written as an aid for construction professionals. Facility owners, project managers and construction superintendents will better understand the challenges as well as the standards for implementing the designated delivery system.

There are three parts to this publication: Part I covers my 68 years of experience and observation in construction. Part II is considered a standalone manual of best practices in construction safety. Part III is for the future (where are we going) with the new technology of artificial intelligence (AI) and the digitized world. I consider Part III to already be obsolete. The technology is changing very fast.

One of the problems with the construction industry is that our macho jobsite personnel feel immune to the risks. Historically, wearing hardhats, tying-on when working at elevated heights, and wearing protective gear was problematic because such requirements were often not mandated prior to the implementation of OSHA in 1971. Today, you still might see a worker riding a crane ball up to an elevated floor or a steelworker handholding steel beams without taglines. However, we have made significant strides in recent years, particularly since 1971, with the implementation of the Occupational Safety and Health Act (OSHA). Currently, job safety meetings are regularly scheduled and the wearing of protective equipment is common. With the carpenter crew of my small construction firm, I remember exerting pressure to wear hardhats. Safety practices were more difficult to achieve before the OSHA Act. Safety issues affect both large projects and small. Small contractors, particularly in the immigration community, are particularly vulnerable to safety issues. The crane industry has changed as equipment capacity has increased and the OSHA Final Rule was established in 2010.

Construction managers are tasked to improve the communication between workers of different nationalities. Today, many Hispanic immigrants arrive speaking only Spanish. Often job site training documents and classes are only in English. On a typical construction site, there may be many employers with different management procedures and workers speaking different languages. Job site management must address this problem. Communication is key to job site safety.

Responsibility to ensure the safety of the construction worker is shared by the owner, the general contractor, construction manager, the employer (possibly a subcontractor) and the architect/engineer (designer). This book addresses the respective responsibilities for construction site safety and crane safety for each of these key players. The owner will establish the overall safety requirement for the project. The designer, through best practices, will task the contractor with the contract documents to prepare a site safety plan. The designer creates a safer project with design for safety. The contractor or construction manager, responsible for means and methods, must manage the project and be the prime party responsible for job site safety.

A Site Safety Plan, including a Crane Safety Plan, represents the best safety practice. The general contractor/construction manager (GC/CM) traditionally coordinates the site safety plan required by the contract documents. Each of the subcontractors will likewise coordinate their own plan and provide input to the GC/CM. The individual trade/subcontracts should require compliance with OSHA and all appropriate regulations. The GC/CM and all subcontractors should ensure that all training is either completed or underway before the job begins and all needed safety equipment is in place.

PART I

SIXTY-EIGHT YEARS OF EXPERIENCE AND OBSERVATION

CHAPTER 1
CONSTRUCTION HISTORY

CONSTRUCTION SAFETY BEFORE OSHA (PRIOR TO 1970)

First Half of Nineteenth Century: No specific safety standards in place.

1817 to 1825: Erie Canal constructed. There were 1000 deaths among the 50,000 workers.

1877: Massachusetts passes first Safety and Health Law. Many safety issues related to factory work such as guards for belts, gears, etc. By 1890, nine states had adopted similar standards.

1883: Brooklyn Bridge completed. There were at least 30 deaths during construction, caused by falls, being hit by loose cables, being caught in drums, getting the bends for workers in the underwater caissons, and becoming trapped under a derrick in the Brooklyn tower. John Roebling, the bridge designer, crushed his foot in a survey incident when his foot was caught between a boat and piling. He died a few weeks later of tetanus. The bridge opened May 1883. It took more than a decade to build. It was the first use of steel rather than iron in bridge construction. After the caissons had been sunk to the river bottom with excavation, they were filled with concrete. Stone towers were erected above to 278 ft above high water. The total cost was about $15 million, twice Roebling's estimate.

Late 1800s: Railroad and mining regulatory commissions were established but had little power and were not effective.

1900s: An average of 300 miners out of every 100,000 workers were killed annually on the job. Workers had to sue employers for damages. Winning was difficult.

2 | BEST PRACTICES IN CONSTRUCTION SITE SAFETY

Lunch atop a Skyscraper, *published in the New York Herald-Tribune, Oct. 2 1932. Photographer unknown.*

1910: New York passed a workers' compensation law. Injuries were compensated at a fixed rate.

1913: The National Safety Council and U.S. Department of Labor were founded.

1916: The Federal Compensation Act created the Office of Workers' Compensation Programs.

1921: Forty four states had adopted workers' compensation laws.

1930: On March 17, construction commenced on the Empire State Building. The 1454 foot building was the highest constructed until the World Trade Center in 1973. From the 3400 workers, there were five deaths. The project finished under budget and ahead of schedule and took twenty months to construct. The foundation was built with two 12-hour shifts. The structural steel was prefabricated. On one 10 day working period 14 floors were erected.

It is fascinating to observe the photos of the steel construction. No hardhats, no tying-on, and workers walking and sitting on steel beams.

1937: The completion of the Golden Gate Bridge saw only 11 fatalities. Ten of these occurred in a single incident when a suspended platform broke. The norm at that time was to expect one fatality for every million dollars spent. The project engineer, Joseph Strauss, turned an important corner for construction site safety. He mandated the requirement to wear hardhats, safety lines, and respirators. This project was the first to use safety nets under the bridge which saved many lives.

1965: Construction on the original World Trade Center commenced and was completed in 1973. There were 60 deaths making a death rate of 17.4/ 1000 workers: a similar rate to the Erie Canal.

1967 Silver Bridge: The bridge was built in 1928 and connected Point Pleasant, West Virginia and Gallipolis, Ohio. On December 15, 1967 at rush hour the bridge collapsed resulting in the death of 46 people. The cause was the failure of a single eye-bar in a suspension chain.

CONSTRUCTION SAFETY AFTER OSHA

December 29, 1970: The William Steiger Occupational Safety and Health Act was signed into law by President Nixon. This led to the establishment of the Occupational Safety and Health Administration (OSHA), the National Institute of Occupational Safety and Health (NIOSH), and the Occupational Safety and Health Review Commission.

April 28, 1971: OSHA was established. It ensured safe working conditions for both construction and general industry.

May 1971: First OSHA Standards which adopted existing national consensus standards.

June 7, 1972: OSHA issues first standard for asbestos. The standard limited workplace exposure to asbestos fibers. Such exposure is now rare. This was significant because construction typically used asbestos insulation.

1972 OSHA State Plans: Plans were approved for South Carolina and Oregon. Currently there are 27 OSHA approved state plans that adopt and enforce OSHA standards.

November 23, 1972: Construction Safety Standards issued for electric power transmission, aerial lifts and helicopters.

January 18, 1978: The roof of the Hartford Civic Center collapsed under a moderately heavy snowstorm. This project is important to mention, not because of construction injuries but for the misuse of a computer assisted design. Fourteen hundred tons of steel and rubble fell on the unoccupied arena below. No one was injured, but there was a basketball game with 5,000 spectators in there shortly before. The roof design featured a state-of-the-art space-frame design. It had few visibility issues and was competitively priced. The roof was assembled on the ground and raised into position. An inspection early on found excessive deflections. There were many complaints about excessive deflection, but the design engineer said that it all was OK. This was a case of overreliance on computer technology. All engineers should know how to check their computations and bear responsibility for their work.

January 29, 1974: Fourteen carcinogens standards established for cancer causing substances.

April 12, 1978: OSHA Training and Education Grants known today as the Susan Harwood Grants. Covers training in high hazard areas. Susan Harwood Grants were given to ASCE for crane safety on construction sites.

April 27, 1978: The Willow Island, West Virginia Disaster. Fifty-one construction workers died when the scaffolding they were working on collapsed at a cooling tower construction site. At the time it was the worst construction disaster in US history.

February 26, 1980: OSHA Coverage for Federal Workers. Executive order issued by President Carter.

July 17, 1981: The Hyatt Regency walkway collapse, Kansas City, Missouri. The hotel had a multi-story atrium with spanned elevated walkways.

The fourth level walkway was aligned directly over the second. A flawed design change resulted in the failure of both walkways which collapsed onto the lobby below. The tie rods for the suspended walkways and their connections were not properly designed and mistakes were made during the shop drawing approval process. One hundred and fourteen people died. The basic question; who was responsible for the design connection and related details? The structural engineer or the fabricator's detailer?

June 28, 1983: The Mianus River Bridge, Greenwich, Conn. A 100-foot-long section on I-95 collapsed into the river below. Three motorists were killed. The National Transportation Safety Board determined that the collapse was caused by the undetected lateral displacement of the hangers of the pin and hanger assembly from corrosion. The State of Connecticut bridge safety inspection and maintenance was faulted.

November 25, 1983: Right to Know Regulations, known as the Hazard Communication Standard. This gives workers the right to know which chemicals they may be exposed to in their workplace. Employers are required to implement a program to train and protect workers.

The material safety data sheet is now basic to all construction sites and is included in required specific training programs.

July 11, 1986: Ground-Fault Circuit Interrupter Standard. OSHA issued the standard for ground-fault circuit protection on construction sites.

April 23, 1987: The L'Ambiance Plaza Collapse, Bridgeport, Connecticut. Twenty-eight workers were killed in this collapse. The project utilized a "lift slab" construction method where the slabs were poured consecutively, stacked and then lifted. This system is rarely used now. There is instability until all the slabs are in place and connected to the columns. A mediation panel was established and all claims for L'Ambiance Plaza were settled at one time. The unusual prompt settlement also ended the investigation. The exact cause of the collapse was never established.

September 1, 1989: Lockout/Tagout Standard issued. Procedures were established to safeguard workers from the unexpected release of hazardous energy.

October 31, 1989: Excavation and Trenching Operations Standard. The shoring of trenches and the provision of access ladders is mandated.

January 14, 1993: OSHA issued a standard which requires safe procedures for entry into confined spaces including manholes, pits, and storage bins

August 9, 1994: Fall Protection Standards require employers to provide safety harnesses and guardrails.

August 39, 1996: Construction Scaffold Safety Standard mandated by OSHA.

January 17, 2001: Steel Erection Standard Issued.

November 15, 2007: Payment for Safety Equipment. OSHA confirmed that owners must pay for most types of personal protective equipment, such as respirators, gloves, etc.

August 9, 2010: OSHA issued the Final Rule on safety for Cranes and Derricks used in construction which replaced 1926.550 regulation.

October 12, 2019: New Orleans Hotel Collapse. The Hard Rock Hotel was under construction when the upper floors collapsed onto lower floors. Two workers were killed and more than thirty were injured. The construction press has not yet indicated a cause. This is included in this book because of the magnitude of the collapse and the problem of two standing tower cranes, without full attachment to the building, and the inherent risk of collapse onto New Orleans Canal Street.

It was announced on October 20, 2019 that a successful controlled demolition explosion separated the jibs and broke the towers in two. The falling cranes landed on the building footprint and the safety risk was solved for New Orleans.

CONCLUSION

Concerning the implementation of OSHA in construction site safety, a comment often heard on the job site is, "We are glad that OSHA has mandated the safe procedures we are to follow." It woke everyone up to their responsibilities.

CHAPTER 2

FORENSIC / LEGAL ASPECTS

There are three aspects of law involving construction: *Common law, Statutory Law* and *Contract Law*. Common law is judge-made law developed over time by precedents in court decisions. Statutory law comes from legislative action by Congress, state legislatures, or municipal bodies. Contract law specifically is the agreement or contract between the construction parties.

The responsibilities of the parties in a construction project are located in the construction documents: general conditions, supplementary conditions, and the drawings and plans. The contract form is probably one of the standard forms: American Institute of Architects (AIA), Engineers Joint Council (EJCDC), or the Associated General Contractors of America (AGC). Modifications to these standard forms are typical in meeting the needs of particular agreements. The court or arbitrator will always look to the contract documents to determine the responsibilities of the parties.

NEGLIGENCE / STANDARD OF CARE

"Negligence Standard" requires a worker to use reasonable care in non-hazardous work. The "absolute standard" will apply an absolute strict liability in a hazardous activity, like blasting, regardless of fault. Construction can often be classified as hazardous. The New York State Scaffold Law would award summary judgment against the owner and contractor in a court decision if an injury to a worker violated the New York Industrial Code.

RESPONSIBILITIES

The parties to a construction project have duties to each other as well as the pedestrians and property owners. A violation results in legal action. Workers are covered by workers' compensation insurance from the employer. The injured worker is compensated even though he or she contributed to the accident. The workers' compensation award, however, is low and does not cover pain and suffering. The injured worker cannot sue the employer, therefore the plaintiff will attempt to find fault with other parties and hold them liable. Only non-employees can sue a contractor.

Supervision and control are the relevant issues where a contractor may be vulnerable to a suit. Owners are seldom liable for construction accidents unless the state requires a "safe place to work" statute. If the owner has retained some of the work supervision, then it might be liable.

DISCOVERY TECHNIQUES

Interrogatories: Written questions are served by one party on the other. The purpose is to determine the legal position of the parties. The party receiving them must serve their answer.

Production and Inspection: A party serves on the adversary a demand for files or physical evidence, i.e. daily reports, minutes of job meetings, photographs, etc.

Depositions: Questions are asked of a witness, under oath, and recorded by a court stenographer. Deposition testimony is a critical element to discovery and strong deposition testimony may lead to settlement.

The procedure has similarities to a trial but there are some key differences: a trial judge will weigh on the testimony and challenges. I found that as an expert witness in a deposition you are more exposed to an aggressive cross examination. There is no judge present and any disputed issue must be subsequently forwarded to the presiding judge for interpretation. The ability of your own lawyer to object is limited.

TRIAL

A trial involves a series of standard steps: opening statements by opposing attorneys, plaintiff's witnesses, direct and cross examination, redirect examination, then the same examinations for the defendant witnesses. Closing arguments by the opposing attorneys follow. The judge then charges the jury with the appropriate law. The jury deliberates and is the sole finder of facts.

ALTERNATIVE DISPUTE RESOLUTION (ADR)

Dispute Review Board (DRB): For large public projects. Disputes are resolved while work is ongoing. The board meets periodically and monitors progress.

MEDIATION

A third party conducts several conferences with the parties in dispute. The mediator provides an atmosphere of reason and can make recommendations. The parties retain control. The mediator first meets with each party and then moves between the opposing sides.

ARBITRATION

The parties agree in advance when an arbitration clause has been placed in the contract. Many contracts reference the American Arbitration Association (AAA). The award determined by the arbitrator or arbitration panel is binding. The admissibility of evidence is different from a court of law. The experience of the arbitrators is significant.

The AAA panels utilize individuals with construction experience who may understand the nuance of the case. The advantage is a simpler procedure compared to the court procedure. I have been a sole arbitrator three times and on arbitration panels several times. As an expert witness, I have not been excluded from the various discussions and would be able to hear directly the opposing side.

FORENSIC ENGINEERING

During the decade of the 1990s I had an active forensic engineering practice in the New York metropolitan area. The definition of this work involved the use of my experience in construction and its application to litigation. You apply your engineering specialty of civil engineering and construction management to issues that may enter or are in the legal arena. I would be retained by the lawyer for either the plaintiff or the defendant in a case. It was important that I balance my time between both plaintiffs and defendants and retain my core business in construction management. This was important so as to not be accused of being a "hired gun."

I had cases that involved general construction issues and construction safety. Falls from scaffolds and ladders were numerous. I was asked to take on as many as four to five new cases a week, many more than I could respond to and investigate. This told me where our safety problems were. Often the wrong ladder was used, such as a residential step ladder rather than a heavier construction type. Or old ladders that broke when used and should have been destroyed, or set at the incorrect angle or inadequate bearing of an extension ladder. There were also too many incorrect ladder uses such as leaning to the side with a heavy tool causing the worker to be unbalanced. An easy solution? Use a scaffold. Scaffold problems, though, were numerous including incorrect setups, using non-scaffold planks which could move or break, non-compatible scaffold parts and absent ladders for access to higher levels. Many problems occurred in the installation and removal of scaffolding. The absence of the complete scaffold requires the worker to "tie on."

In a similar vein, based upon the quantity of cases, I was made more aware of the risks of unprotected skylight, stairwells, and other openings. It is essential that roofing work protect the skylight openings with a cover or guardrail immediately if there is a time delay before the skylight is installed.

Other construction activities that I consulted:
- Single steps and ramps without handrails. A single step should have at least a handrail to both assist the individual and to flag the impending change of level.
- Material falling from work onto other workers or the public.
- Electric lock/tag out where it is necessary to control latent potential energy.
- Construction quality. A disappointed project owner will sue for a faulty installation.
- Blasting is used in demolition and the resulting vibrations create collateral damage to adjacent structures.
- Excavation, particularly trenching. The need to use a trench guard or to taper the side slope is often overlooked when the need to complete a pipe connection is required. The temptation to violate the five-foot rule of trench depth must be resisted. This violation would have tragic results.
- Roofing work with hot tar. The issue of falling while walking with buckets of hot roofing material is all too common. A transporter

should be used or a clear tar free walkway should be available.
- Street traffic controls: Urban work on city streets requires barricades, signage and lighting. A car running through a barricade is a serious problem.
- Construction equipment. Hand saws, pneumatic staplers, and jackhammers all have instruction manuals and standards of operation.
- Cranes: This has been a sub specialty of mine and is covered in more depth in Chapter 3 which emphasizes the training and certification issues along with the responsibilities of the lift director and the other participants. Many of my forensic cases involved the crane overturning. An overturn occurs where the load is too great for the crane configuration which could be due to inadequate training in the use of the load chart. There are also other factors such as incorrect use of outriggers and poor ground support.

What was the process of accepting a case? I would receive an inquiry from a lawyer asking me to be an expert on behalf of his or her client. If my instinct was OK, I then sent a letter contract to be signed and I asked for a retainer. The amount of the retainer varied with the complexity of the case, but it would be at least the value of four hours of my normal fee. Until the agreement was signed, I was not retained. At that point, I felt comfortable in proceeding to review the documentation and perform a site visit, but my full evaluation and opinion could only be reached with a complete review. There were occasions when my opinion did not meet the expectations of the requesting lawyer and I separated from the case.

Most accidents were evaluated by reading the accident reports, depositions, and all reports on the record. If at all possible, I would go to the site, hopefully before conditions were altered. It was important that I always asked for this opportunity even though the time to investigate the site would add to my billing.

COURT CASES REVIEWED

I have testified in the following cases which are representative of my courtroom experience:

Chiarelli v. 128 Eighth Ave. Plaintiff Chiarelli fell 10 feet from a collapsed platform designated to catch debris. The judge directed a verdict under the NY Scaffold Law. Verdict $221,000. I testified for the plaintiff: Chiarelli should not have been required to work on the platform. The Scaffold Law will automatically award to the plaintiff under a fall from a working platform.

Zhagnay v. Royal Realty. Plaintiff was demolishing a 20-foot-high masonry wall when it fell on him. Scaffolding was not supplied for him to demolish from the top. Further, he was told to proceed from the bottom. I testified for the defendant that the plaintiff was responsible and should have known not to demolish from the bottom. This looks like common sense, but I always try to determine the past training of the injured worker. Judges directed verdict: $950,400 under Labor Law 240 and 241(6).

Gonzalez v. Anglebrook Limited. The plaintiff, a 37-year-old laborer, fell when descending a scaffold. He fell 25 feet descending from the top platform. I testified for the plaintiff. No stairs or ladder was provided. Plaintiff was climbing down the scaffold frame. Settlement of $775,000 under Labor Law 240 and 241(6).

Flood v. City of New York. Flood, a 39 year old ironworker, was working on the NY Manhattan Bridge for the general contractor. A girder being hoisted was stuck and he was working to free it. The girder shifted, falling a short distance, and Flood's ankle was caught in a cable and he injured his shoulder while preventing a fall. Because of the short fall of the girder, the court directed a verdict under Labor Law 240. Settlement for the plaintiff was $3,000,000. I testified for the plaintiff.

Bellinzoni v. Birgir Seland. The plaintiff was working on the mezzanine of a warehouse when his foot broke through the plywood floor. He fell 12 feet off the exposed level without guard rails. I testified for the plaintiff that the mezzanine was not built to code: there was inadequate flooring and no guardrail. The judge threw out my testimony because I was "an engineer, not a carpenter." This was my only experience where my testimony was not accepted. An appeal was made, and the judge was directed to accept my testimony. When the case reconvened Judge Murphy treated me with unusual respect.

Lentini v. Tishman, Crimmins. Lentini, a 61 year-old construction worker, fell into a trench from an "A" frame ladder while hanging tarp onto a sidewalk bridge. I testified for the plaintiff. The ladder was set up next to the trench which was not shored or braced. Verdict: $330,000.

Vals v. Lombardi. The plaintiff, 61 year-old woman, lived in an apartment adjacent to one being renovated. Structural vibrations cause the plaster ceiling to fall onto her face. I testified for the plaintiff. I explained how the structural vibrations weakened an archway causing the collapse. Verdict $600,000.

McCoy v. MTA. This was a case where a Gradall (or telehandler) was used as a crane. It is a forklift, but with a telescoping boom and suspended hook so that it can be configured like a crane. I testified for the Plaintiff that the Gradall, as a multipurpose machine defined by OSHA, when configured as a crane, must follow the regulations for a functioning crane. The verdict concluded that the machine meets the intent of the New York State Industrial code for cranes which requires taglines and keeping the area clear. McCoy and co-workers were transporting a 20-foot I-beam on Manhattan Park Avenue suspended from the Gradall boom. There was no tagline. Mr. McCoy hand-held the right side of the beam. When the machine stopped for a red light and the beam swung forward and back, a wheel ran over his foot. This brought the case to Labor Law 241(6) and a violation of the New York State Industrial Code.

Lane v. SKC Auburndale. This is another case of a telehandler being used as a crane. The case addressed New York Labor Law 240. The definition of a crane was not the issue. The liability was determined by the slippage of the cable from the machine due to the inadequate cable clamp on a beam that was being lowered into position in a below grade bank vault. The falling beam impacted Mr. Kane's foot. I prepared an affidavit indicating that the beam was not properly rigged and a proper application of Labor Law 240.

Cavanaugh v. Township of Montclair. I was an expert on behalf of the defendant, Township Montclair, NJ. The contractor, Cavanaugh, claimed that the Township Montclair, the owner, had caused a delay and the case and was involved in an extensive arbitration proceeding. The cost of construction was carefully discussed. I developed a cost analysis of the entire Cavanaugh work. This was done in a "reverse review" using the contractor's daily reports and payroll information. I had a computer program that would develop cost reports from payroll input that we used with our own carpenters and laborers. I ended up with reports on the Cavanaugh contractor's actual costs. I felt more prepared than the plaintiff's supporters.

Powell v. City of New York, New York Dormitory Authority. Mr. Powell was a steel worker on a raising gang erecting steel framing at Jacobi Medical Center, Bronx, New York. Mr. Powell was straddling a steel beam of the sixth-floor framing and was tied off to the same beam. A beam was lifted from the fourth floor to be installed on the sixth. As it was being lifted it impacted the fifth-floor framing and severed the tag line. The beam was 15-20 feet above Powell and out of control. The steel beam came down and hit Powell on his back, raised up, and fell again on his shoulder. I found several problems. The load should not be allowed to be hoisted over workmen. It should always be in control, not allowed to swing freely and impact structures and workers. Powell's lifeline should have been tied off to a safety cable that would allow him some movement to avoid the swinging beam. The lift should have stopped when the load first impacted the fifth floor. The lack of a tag line was critical. I prepared an affidavit as the plaintiff's expert.

Rusi v. Park See Assoc. Rasim Rusi was employed to perform roofing work on Park Avenue in Manhattan, N.Y. His job was to place hot tar from a bucket and then spread it with a mop. It was his second day on the job. I testified for the plaintiff. My position was that he was not properly trained or instructed. He was tasked to walk through a series of dunnage beams. He decided on his own to walk on the beams. He fell off and was severely burned with the hot tar. Rusi should have been provided with a scaffolding over the dunnage or a clear walking path. A settlement awarded for $325,000.

Note: This is similar to the Manuel Perez case below. The walkway in a roofing job must be clear and safe. Proper training was lacking in both cases.

"Manuel Perez" v. City of New York: I testified in a case involving a Mexican immigrant, Manuel Perez (not his actual name). Manuel had only attended two years of grade school in Mexico. He had a smattering of jobs in the New York construction industry. In the case in question he was a laborer on a roof installation project in New York City carrying hot tar. He tripped and fell due to the fact that that the runway on the roof was coated with the asphalt roofing material which stuck to his shoes. He was also not wearing the proper protective clothing and was badly burned when he fell. He received severe burns when the bucket of hot asphalt he was carrying splashed onto his face and arms.

Proper procedures would involve not allowing the buildup of the adhesive asphalt material on the walking runway, using transportable equipment, and wearing proper protective clothing. Manuel was given some safety lectures in English with handouts in both Spanish and English. I was able to interview Manuel in Spanish and discovered that he was illiterate in both English and Spanish. He was not able to read the safety handouts in either language. He certainly did not understand the lectures in English, one of which involved asphalt roofing. The final settlement of the case emphasized the inadequate supervision and the lack of a transporter to move the material. In my mind, the poor communications and training of this Mexican immigrant laborer contributed significantly to the incident.

James Jones v. Edgewater Park: On September 10, 1997, I inspected a building in the Bronx, New York known as The Mansion. Mr. Jones fell off the roof of the apparatus room of the firehouse, an extension of The Mansion. I recently (March 31, 2020) was deposed on my findings of September 10, 1997 when I was retained by the defendant, Edgewater Park. On September 4, 1993 Mr. Jones was attending a social event in The Mansion. He left the event and went onto the adjacent roof of the apparatus room and fell off the unprotected roof edge. This case involved building code, not construction issues. It is interesting in that my affidavit surfaced and was addressed in my deposition of March 31, 2020. I am a fact witness to the conditions in 1997. There was a later fall accident and legal case with similar conditions which subsequently have changed. The building code issues involved the functioning of a locked gate leading to the roof and the requirement for roof parapets in New York City. Because of the 2020 virus pandemic, I was deposed using the video conferencing platform Zoom which enabled the court reporter, three lawyers, and I to stay in our homes in front of our computers. An interesting experience using the latest technology.

OVERVIEW

It should be noted that I testified for both plaintiffs and defendants. It was always *my opinion* that I presented in court. I never became an advocate for the individual. In order to present this image, I would leave the courtroom as quickly as possible and not talk with the individual plaintiff or defendant.

One interesting court event occurred when the attorney client introduced me, he referenced the documents that had been forwarded for my review. I realized that there were three key differences from my list. I was always careful to have the documents that I received recognized because that would be the grounds for my opinion. In this particular case, I stated to the judge (and jury) that I could not testify since I had not been presented with three of the documents. I showed up at 8:00 a.m. for the start of the following day's proceedings. The entire court, with jury in the box, sat for two hours as I read the missing information. I then continued my testimony as it did not change my opinion. This brings up an important issue: I always insisted that I receive all information and documentation. Only then could I render an opinion. Occasionally, if an attorney client held back items, it was possibly an effort to put a particular spin on the record and opinion. At other times it may have been an effort to reduce my preparation time and cost.

The question of worker responsibility can be very sensitive. I always took the position that it was important to know of the training and experience of the injured worker. It is too easy to lose sight of this principle when the discussion of the incident addresses code and safety violations of the facility. I expect a trained and experienced worker to bear some responsibility.

There were some cases where my opinion addressed the responsibility of one participant, say the construction manager in a case where there was an injured subcontractor's worker. The worker had a good case and my job was to provide an opinion in the defense of the CM after reviewing its management practices at the site. I would investigate and conclude if there was oversight responsibility on the part of the CM.

ETHICS IN THE COURT ROOM

My practice in forensic work was from 1986 to 2007 in the New York City Metropolitan area. I have been qualified to give expert testimony in over 100 cases.

As a professional engineer, we are held to a high standard of ethics and holding to the truth. As a member of The National Academy of Forensic Engineers (NAFE), the standard requiring truthful testimony was emphasized. NAFE is a society of professional engineers in forensic investigation and litigation support.

Here are my thoughts on some unethical lawyers I have had contact with. On a few occasions, I arrived at the courthouse anticipating I would provide testimony in a case. During the last minute "prep" by the attorney, I was asked to say something either not true or contrary to my findings. I said "no" and then went home. I have also observed lawyers that will bring suit or abuse witnesses for unethical advantage. In theory, the legal system protects both sides of the litigation given equally capable lawyers, etc. The unethical lawyer was a problem only when I first entered forensic practice. My office developed a system of flagging an individual in our database of lawyers (with addresses) when it was decided that I would never work for him or her. As time went on and my reputation for honesty took hold, I became selective to only working for ethical lawyers. The request for untruthful testimony disappeared. I also determined that I had no need to continue advertising.

I have always strived to be ethical and truthful. My opinions were my own and not reflective of the money I received. The opposing attorney might attempt to call me a "hired gun." Unfortunately, the reputation of some witnesses is not good. Many are not professional engineers and perhaps their profession is not exacting in its ethics. In the New York State Supreme Court, I would provide testimony and leave, not normally allowed to observe the other witnesses. On occasion you might be given the transcript of witnesses on the other side and have the opportunity for rebuttal. It is preferable, in most instances, to immediately depart the court room after testimony so as to present the image of being independent and not motivated by the outcome. In other words, "not an advocate" for one side.

There were some venues where it was normal to hear the other witnesses such as arbitration hearings, local town courts, and the New York

State Court of Claims. The latter heard cases where a state agency was a party to the litigation. I was often surprised by the lack of independence and truthfulness of many expert witnesses I heard, often memorizing their lawyer's tutored expressions.

It was important for me to have experience with both the plaintiffs and defendants. An expert witness that only works for one side can be accused of bias. It was also important that I continue with my engineering consultant work and construction management business. It will enhance your professional credibility if you are not working full time as an expert witness. I never was a full-time expert witness. The opposing attorney would not hesitate to try to make you into a "hired gun" if you were not active in your professional practice.

THE ACCIDENT / FORENSIC INVESTIGATION

The management objective should be to learn from our mistakes. This is not easily done as it requires participants to openly discuss the events and find methods of improvement even self-criticism. Then add the element of litigation. Management and the firm's lawyer will "circle the wagons" and expect everyone to admit nothing. There are two types of accident Investigations:

1. The accident investigation that is performed to determine actual cause and to implement remediation to prevent subsequent occurrences.
2. The forensic investigation that looks for facts which may lead to litigation. The report will likely be sent to an attorney.

There is obviously a similarity in the two approaches which are trying to find the cause of the incident. The accident investigation is able to look inward to the operating organization and evaluate what went wrong, asking, "when," "how," and "why." This is translated into an action plan to be sure it does not repeat. The National Safety Council states, "accident investigation and analysis is one of the means to prevent accidents." The forensic investigation looks at the incident from the perspective of possible litigation. My experience is almost completely forensic. There is a certain "circle the wagons" following an accident when a contractor cannot be forthwith because of potential litigation, particularly when their own staff was complicit in the incident. I adhere to the standards of the National Academy of Forensic Engineers (NAFE): "The role of the forensic engineer is that of an impartial scientist who strives to obtain truth through scientific inquiry, employing the tools of the scientific method and his/her engineering expertise."

CHAPTER 3
SPECIFICS TO CRANE SAFETY DEVELOPMENT

The crane industry has evolved considerably over the past century. Derricks and hoisting equipment have been married to carriers: trucks and crawlers. The first code of crane safety standards was promulgated by the American Society of Mechanical Engineers (ASME) in 1916. World War I saw the development of cranes as we know them. The capacity, speed, and reach of operation increased. At the end of World War II, cranes used lattice type booms and power changed from steam to gas and diesel engines. By the 1950s, hydraulic clutches replaced friction systems. Telescoping booms were developed. High strength steel increased boom capacity. Boom trucks, cranes with articulated booms and tower cranes, were developed. The operations have now been enhanced with the development of computers and electronic devices.

The past two decades have seen significant changes in the crane industry. New OSHA regulations have been established and industry standards such as ASME B30.5[1] have been updated to enhance safety.

I was fortunate to be a part of this process. I was chairman of the Crane Safety Committee of the American Society of Civil Engineers (ASCE) which took a lead in crane safety issues. On November 28, 1989, a tower crane collapsed in San Francisco. Five people were killed and twenty-two were injured. On August 31, 1990, the ASCE President John A. Focht appointed a Task Committee on Crane Safety on Construction Sites to develop an ASCE Policy for Crane Safety. I was appointed chairman of the committee.

The composition of the Committee was significant for the level of experience on construction and crane safety and usage:

---

1 See "American Society of Mechanical Engineers (ASME) B30 Committe" in Chapter 4 for further discussion on the ANSI ASME B30 Committee.

- Harlan W. Fair, Chairman: Consulting Engineer for Construction
- Joseph Kaplan, Contractor: Construction Division EXCOM Contact
- Howard I. Shapiro, Consulting Engineer-Cranes: Chairman ANSI B30.4
- Patrick E. Galuso, Project Engineer: Crane Manufacturer
- Paul S. Zorich, Chief Consultant Cranes: Naval Facilities Engineering Command (NAVFAC)

Chairman ANSI B30
- William R. Nash, Contractor: ASCE Equipment and Techniques Committee
- Dwight B. Sale, Consultant Heavy Construction: Retired VP Guy F. Atkinson Co.
- Matthew J. Burkart, Consultant Cranes: Chairman ANSI A10
- Philip J. Alterman, Consulting Forensic Engineer: Crane Accident Investigations

The Task Committee became the standing Crane Safety Committee which investigated and developed the responsibilities of the crane owner, designer, contractor crane operator, lift director and riggers. We had three active participants with the ASME B30 Committee. Paul Zorich was the chairman, Howard Shapiro was the chairman of B30.4 (Portal and Pedestal Cranes) and I became Paul Zorich's alternate. The B30.5 Standard had been regarded as the bible for mobile cranes. A B30.5 sub-committee was assigned to investigate the responsibilities of the job site crane operations. We participated in these discussions. The 2007 edition of ASME B30.5 introduced, for the first time, a listing of key responsibilities, including: crane owner, crane user, site supervisor, lift director, and crane operator. The lift director had now received national recognition.

The ASCE Crane Task Committee participated in the OSHA cranes and derricks negotiated rulemaking in 2004. We submitted written comments to the draft regulatory text and participated in the public comments. Advisory Committee (CDAC).

The OSHA Cranes and Derricks in Construction Final Rule was released in the Federal Register in 2010. Under Sec 1926.1432 Multiple-Lifts, a lift director is assigned to review the lift plan. During the period of comments, the ASCE Crane Safety Committee recommended to OSHA that the new regulation should include the lift director.

CHAPTER 4
EXPERIENCE

1952, New Orleans Grain Elevator: I mention this because it was my first construction job. With some surveying instruction as a Junior at Dartmouth College, I was assigned to setting pile cut-off grades. The danger of my new industry was driven home when I saw a worker who was severely injured when trapped in the leads of a pile driver. Hard hats were not mandated and worn sporadically.

1955-1957, Active Duty Navy Civil Engineer Corps: I was in charge of special projects at Reserve Training Centers 5th Naval District and Maintenance Office at the Naval Air Station Argentia, Newfoundland. The Argentia assignment was my first real job following Dartmouth College and Thayer School of Engineering. I had to grow up fast as I was challenged from the start. A Seabee detachment was assigned to me headed by eight World War II chiefs. They either got me in trouble, but most probably kept this brand-new Ensign out of trouble. The civilian maintenance force was also assigned to me along with the officers mess (BOQ).

An interesting anecdote: There were three separate construction organizations in Argentia: My public works department with both civilian and Seabees, a regular Seabee Construction Battalion, and a major civilian contractor under a Navy Civil Engineer Corps construction group. Each organization had its own distinct supply system. We were an overseas operation and one had to anticipate your needs well in advance. It did not always work out in the ideal manner. I developed a ledger sheet that managed the distribution of bags of cement among the three entities. If we loaned 50 bags to the battalion, I made that entry and that became their obligation to repay at some point. The Seabees and Civil Engineer Corps became expert in "cumshaw"; — how to find things you need in the system. Bags of cement became a medium of exchange. You might pay say for a table saw if you had sufficient bags of cement.

The 1964 NY World's Fair

1964, New York World's Fair: I was Project Engineer for Thompson Starrett Construction Company for the New York state exhibit. We all wore hardhats. The World's Fair management sponsored regular safety meetings; all exhibit contractors were required to attend. I held safety meetings for the New York state exhibit project with all subcontractors in attendance. The site safety challenge was the extensive work at heights. Each of the towers was constructed with slip form technology where concrete was placed continuously into a vertically moving form for the entire height of the structure. The soffits under the three observation towers were stucco finished with workers on high scaffolds. The New York state exhibit realized one significant fall accident by an electrician.

The large steel supports for the cable suspended pavilion roof were fabricated by Ingalls Iron in Birmingham, Alabama. In 1963, I traveled to Birmingham to inspect the status of the fabrication. This was in the middle of the civil rights demonstrations: the infamous Bull Connor with his fire hoses and the church bombing. Jackie Robinson and Floyd Patterson, the notable black athletes, were passengers on my plane. They were providing their support to the civil rights effort. There was one demonstration at the New York state exhibit by black tradesmen attempting to gain entry into the construction unions. The history of this effort has the same timeframe of the civil rights effort in the 1960s. My outlook on construction opportunity for Black and Hispanic workers is from New York. Major construction was done under collective bargaining; i.e. union jobs. Diversity centered on how workers became apprentices in

the construction unions. In the 1960s, New York was in a construction boom, not just the World's Fair. Discriminatory hiring had given 92 percent building trade members to the white work force. Today (2020) the black workers represent 22.2 percent in the union construction workforce and 15.8 percent in non-union hiring.

A Timeline of the Civil Rights Movement
- February 1, 1960: Woolworth lunch counter protest in Greensboro, N.C.
- May 4, 1961: Freedom Riders protested segregation of southern bus terminals.
- August 28, 1963: March on Washington to force civil rights legislation.
- 1964: Civil Rights Act signed by President Johnson.
- August 6, 1965: President Johnson signed the Voting Rights Act.
- April 4, 1968: Martin Luther King assassinated.

The above photo is of the nearly completed New York state project. The extensive scaffolding beneath the three distinctive towers has an interesting history. The project architect was Phillip Johnson, a famous and prestigious individual who was used to getting his way. The soffits under the towers were very high off the ground, and plastering was by far the expensive option. I did some research on raising prefabricated panels from above. Phillip Johnson was not impressed. He did not want the visible lines of the panel separations. He insisted that the exposed soffits be plastered. I remember the job meeting and we (including the owner and the State of New York representative), expressed to Johnson, "do we have to?" He said yes and that was the end of the discussion. Another sidelight. I "bought" the necessary scaffolds as they became available from another World's Fair Thompson Starrett job. We then became the installation subcontractor for the scaffolding needed to plaster the three tower platform soffits.

1968, Cornell Medical School, at New York Hospital:

Harkness Medical Research Building: I was the owner's representative for the construction of the Harkness Medical Research Building, dedicated in 1968. Each of the Harkness research modules was of a fixed size with masonry walls. This concept has changed in medical and engineering labs to an open flexible area with multi-disciplined investigators. The job site safety challenge was in the deep construction of the basement and elevator shafts in wet groundwater from broken city water mains. Foundation and elevator pit waterproofing was significant.

I was the construction mer for The Cornell Medical School and New York Hospital.

Cornell Medical Group: One project involved moving the Cornell Medical Group from their research lab at the old Bellevue Hospital to the satellite building, Kips Bay, on 69th Street. All of the lab equipment, casework, and desks were removed from Bellevue and set at Kips Bay. I was in charge of moving Dr. Tom Almy and his group. We left only the old counter tops supported by 2x4s. The Dean of Cornell Medical received an angry message from Bernie Weinstein, CEO of Bellevue, that we had illegally taken medical equipment from Bellevue. I met with Bernie Weinstein and he chewed me out that once equipment is in place in the hospital, it belongs to the city of New York. This was probably legally correct, but it was difficult for the Cornell investigators to understand because the items were purchased with their grant funds. I met with Dep. Commissioner of Hospitals Bob Derzon, a Dartmouth classmate, over lunch and agreed this should be put to bed. I instructed Turner Construction Corp, my contractor, to clean up the Bellevue site.

The NYC Deptartment of Hospitals later became the Health and Hospital Corp (HHC). I was recruited by Derzon to join HHC. When

I would run into Bernie Weinstein in capital budget reviews he would shake his finger at me for stealing his equipment.

1970, New York City Health and Hospital Corp (HHC) acquired Bellevue Hospital. I was Director of Project Management for HHC and part of the team to receive the new Bellevue Hospital, at the completion of construction, from NYC Public Works. The job of my project management team was to monitor projects throughout the city hospital system and to assist in the development of capital budgets for each hospital.

1980s, West Point contracts by H. Fair Assoc.: Modifications to Shea Stadium, addition and alteration to fire house, Alteration Eisenhower Hall, and addition to the Post Exchange. The only injury and law suit filed against H. Fair Assoc., Inc. was to a pedestrian at the West Point Fire House. There was an excavated pit bordered by a high mound of earth. The individual was not in a designated pedestrian area and climbed up and over the mound and fell into the excavation. He claimed injuries. The legal case went nowhere. At the time I thought our protection adequate, but an added barrier would have given a clearer signal to not trespass.

I competitively bid on all the work at West Point with one exception. I would complete my bid, to the extent possible, before driving the 40 minutes to West Point when the bid was due. I would then call back to the office from a phone booth (before cell phones). To see if any late sub bids were received. With one final review, I then submitted the bid. I used my own carpenter and labor crews so a major portion of the bid was my estimate. Labor rates were fixed in that all bidders were on the same cost level because it was mandatory to use the area rates.

Some of my labor were the college age children from our Chappaqua, NY base. My sons always wanted to work at West Point because the rate was higher than Westchester County. We had to submit certified payrolls to West Point. In addition, my union carpenters required the submission of payroll information to the union local jurisdiction for their "stamps" (vacation coverage). Our payroll computer software was able to use as many as three jurisdictions for any payroll period. The one negotiated contract at West Point was the construction of the concrete parade reviewing stand donated by a West Point class.

Construction Management: I was Project Manager for Xerox on the construction of a consumables plant in Oklahoma City that manufactured toner and consumables for Xerox equipment. J.A. Jones was the construction manager (CM). The pre-construction project development was enlightening in that Oklahoma City was so open and helpful through all approvals, a very different experience from east coast development. I was resident at the jobsite with a staff of inspectors and flew home to Westchester County every weekend. My family joined me for the summer in my Oklahoma apartment which was a great opportunity to see the west. Also resident on site were Xerox auditors who were particularly tough on reviewing requisitions and the guaranteed max price (GMP) with the CM.

Two Condominium Projects used the CM contracts at risk. I sponsored condominium projects in Pelham Manor and Chappaqua N.Y. Planning Board approval was most difficult, as contrasted to the Oklahoma experience. The Pelham Manor job involved renovating two old apartment buildings. I planned to put in elevators and bring them totally to code. It was hard to understand the residents' resistance when the project involved removing a ghetto in an upscale community. One building was "torched" by an arsonist. I had listed the second building with the National Historic Register. I was intrigued in the fine historical detail of 19th Century construction and it gave some resistance to mounting pressure to remove the building.

I completed the project by getting approval for five high end duplex buildings architecturally patterned after the local single family units. The Chappaqua project also received community resistance even though it also was an improvement to the substandard construction in an otherwise upscale community. H. Fair Assoc. Inc., my construction firm, utilized a CM contract. I was double hatted in that I was the sponsor of these projects as well as the CM.

Design-Build: When I was a Project Manager for Xerox, I had one design-build contract, a warehouse in Indianapolis. Many school construction projects are design-build. As a small CM with my own business I would often wrap the design of a residential addition within my contact. That was always a simplified design. Governor Cuomo of New York was very visible in advocating design-build for the Tappan Zee replacement build project.

The super crane used in dismantling the Tappan Zee Bridge, nicknamed "I Lift NY."

Currently (2020) two replacement long span bridges are under construction on I-91 in Vermont utilizing a design-build delivery system.

Modular and Off-Site Construction: The potential for increased safety is significant; however, I reviewed two forensic cases where there were serious injuries due to the same problem: the roof collapsed on a worker on an off-site constructed house. One was in New York and the other in Vermont. The single-family residences were constructed off site and dropped by crane on the pre-constructed foundation. The roofs lay in a flat position and the crane assignment was to lift the roof to the final slope by attaching the hook to the ridge beam. Before the crane released the roof, a construction worker had to place bracing below to support the roof. Unfortunately, the ridge nailing was not designed for the procedure and it pulled apart thereby releasing the roof to fall upon the worker. These were cases where the design was faulty and/or the instructions with the modular building were inadequate. The experience and knowledge of the crane operator and contractor's superintendent were questionable. The injuries were serious.

Diversity in Construction: The Thayer School of Engineering at Dartmouth College (my engineering school) graduated more women engineers in 2018 than men, the first in the nation to do so.

In my other life as a retired navy captain, Civil Engineer Corps, I recognize the elevation of RADM Katherine Gregory in 2014 as the first woman to lead the Civil Engineer Corps (CEC). As chief of civil engineers she was in charge of all construction by the Naval Facilities Engineering Command as well as the Navy Seabee battalions. In my active time in the CEC there were no women CEC officers. A good friend in the CEC was Wes Brown. He was the first African-American to graduate from the Naval Academy. I was assigned to his public works department for training duty at Floyd Bennett Field, New York.

In 2018, the publication the Engineering News Record (ENR) completed a comprehensive survey, "Speaking Out," with 1248 women respondents. A percentage of 36.2 said they experienced sexual harassment on a construction job site. It was both inappropriate questions and innuendo as well a physical contact. ENR concluded that the industry is predisposed to workplace sexual harassment due to gender disparity, marginalization, macho culture, normalized behavior, and outdated attitudes. My take is the strong machismo in construction. From another perspective, a woman friend who is both a civil engineer and an owner of apartment houses, manages her own construction projects. As both owner and contractor, she often is confronted by machismo resistance to what normally is a decision to proceed. When she talks the workplace vernacular, "you're f......ng right, that's what I want." Then the work moves ahead.

Surveying provided me with the skills to work on the job site in construction and as an aid to run a small business. In the summer of 1953, I worked with the State of California Highways surveying on freeways in Los Angeles. My first civilian job, with Turner Construction, involved line and grade for buildings under construction. I bought a transit and level from the Thayer School which was used as my personal equipment on projects with H. Fair Associates. I did all lay-out work on the projects in Westchester County. The transit was a classic early 20th Century brass instrument originally donated to Thayer by a late 19th Century Thayer School graduate (last name Snow). It was more accurate than the normal builder's instrument. It required a special skill in that it had an inverted lens. The image was upside-down when looking through the scope. No one else on my staff would use the instrument. They could not adjust to the inverted lens. I recently donated it back to Thayer School for its archive. Today, surveying is different with the use of lasers in leveling and instruments that retain the reading and transmit the data to a computer. The drudgery of computing offsets is done with computer software. At Thayer School, we learned to properly enter data to the field book. It was emphasized that it might become a legal document.

Politics: There was always politics in both the corporate business world and the Navy. This involved protecting your turf or jurisdiction and socializing with dinner invitations, but it was most important to treat your clients well. As maintenance officer in Argentia, I had control of funds and resources for many small and moderate sized projects. I was correctly educated in the field of scheduling: the best way to efficiently complete the work is a first in-first out sequence. However, the base executive officer and department heads outranked me and wanted their projects done "yesterday." I learned that I had to convince these special clients that I will be on their project as fast as possible and still try to balance the remaining work because the lower ranked requests were also my clients. At New York Hospital, the department heads were in a similar position of strength and "yesterday" often was not soon enough. All construction has clients that will occupy or benefit from the project's completion. I always kept that in mind and tried to make them feel that I had their interest at heart. The real client is the user, not necessarily the person awarding you the job. In the above example at Cornell Medical and New York Hospital the real client was Dr. Tom Almy and his medical team, not the Cornell Dean or Bellevue Hospital.

CHAPTER 5
CONSTRUCTION DELIVERY SYSTEMS

DESIGN-BID-BUILD

Design-bid-build is the traditional delivery method. There are three sequential phases: Design, Bidding, and Construction.

DESIGN PHASE: An architect or engineer is retained by the owner to design the building or infrastructure. The designer works with the owner to determine the requirement and prepares a program. Other professionals work with the designer, structural engineer, mechanical engineer, and a landscape architect. A schematic phase is developed and then the final construction drawings are prepared for bidding.

BID PHASE: General contractors will receive bid documents and will prepare a bid including sub-contractor bids. It is best practice to pre-qualify the bidders. If this is done the award will most likely go to the low bidder. If all of the bids are over the project budget, the designer may be instructed to revise the bid documents.

CONSTRUCTION PHASE: The successful general contractor proceeds with the project. The designer (architect or engineer) works as the owner's agent to approve requisitions for payment and review work progress.

Limitations: There is a cheap mentality on the part of the bidders and subcontractors with following disputes. The general contractor is brought into the process after the construction documents are complete. There is no opportunity to have the general contractor discuss constructability or provide options during the design. The designer may not be knowledgeable on construction costs and methodology.

CONSTRUCTION MANAGEMENT

The traditional method of construction was for the project owner to hire an architect or architect and engineer (A&E) to design the project. After the design completion, the project was put out to bid. The lowest bid was awarded the job. The management of the project abruptly shifted from the design professional to the contractor. But it was the lack of good management in the delivery system that was the catalyst to create the construction management (CM) delivery system. The relationship between the owner and the general contractor (GC) was often adversarial. The GC motivation was to complete the job with low costs to maximize profits. The owner's motivation was to extract the most possible within the contract cost.

In the 1960s there was significant construction activity with the national highway system. The inflation rate was often in double digits and delays in construction were costly. The World Trade Center, commenced in 1966, was the first publicized use of CM. The Federal General Services Administration (GSA) had published a report in the 1960's recommending the use of CM.

In the 1970's the Associated General Contractors (AGC) published guidelines that defined a CM as a qualified GC, selected at the same time as the architect, to work during the planning and design phase for a fee. The AGC has defined the CM role to have a guaranteed maximum price and with the possibility of doing some of the work with their own forces. The American Institute of Architects (AIA) designated the CM as a professional agent of the owner; the owner had management oversight of the trade contracts.

A task Committee was formed in 1974 by the American Society of Civil Engineers (ASCE) to better define the roles of the owner, designer and CM. H. Fair was a member of this committee. The CM was defined as an entity that worked with the owner and designer from the beginning, making recommendations on design improvements and construction technology.

The AGC, AIA, and Engineers Joint Council have produced documents that can be used for contracts in projects utilizing the CM delivery system.

CONSTRUCTION MANAGER AT RISK

The Construction Manager at Risk is a delivery system where the CM must deliver the project within a guaranteed maximum price (GMP). The CM acts as a consultant to the owner during the design phase. The CM will establish a cost model for the project. All design options will be estimated and reviewed for constructability. If possible, a GMP will be established prior to final bidding at the sub-contractor level. Sub-contractor bids might also be received at the various stages of design completion. The CM at risk is an owner's advocate. It is important to realize that the GMP is based upon the design drawings. Any scope increase will be followed by a change order to increase the GMP.

CONSTRUCTION MANAGER AS ADVISOR

The Construction Manager as Advisor or agent is a delivery system where a professional (the CM) is a prime consultant to the owner. The contractor and architect also report directly to the owner. The CM will advise the owner on construction matters during the design and construction phases. AIA documents A132, B132, and C132 are used for owner contracts with trade contractors, the architect and CM.

The CM in both the At Risk and Advisor (owner's agent) performs as owners advocate during the design phase. The CM role during the construction phase is different, but the CM will always have the owner's best interest. The traditional design-bid-build delivery system required the design to be complete before bidding commenced and the bidding to be complete before construction was awarded. Under a CM procedure, it is possible to fast track or commence construction before all design is complete. Under this concept, bid packages can be scheduled that will allow construction to proceed while design continues.

DESIGN-BUILD

Design-Build is a delivery system where there is just one entity that performs the function of design and construction. The owner hopes that it will reduce risks and costs. I understand that historically this represents the oldest delivery system, the "master builder." I call the design-bid-build the traditional system, but design-build actually preceded it, and it would be more accurate to give it that recognition.

This delivery system can be led by either a designer, contractor, or a joint venture of a designer and contractor. Advocates of design-build state that time and money is saved. Construction can commence earlier and overlap the design process. Errors and omissions are readily resolved with the single entity responsibility. The owner cannot be caught between the designer and the contractor. The overlapping of the construction with the design makes it an alternative to the CM fast track approach.

MODULAR AND OFFSITE CONSTRUCTION

Modular and off-site construction are not new. There is a new emphasis because of the labor shortage in 2019. The use of building components off-site relieves the pressure to staff the site with ample workers. There is also increased efficiency in bringing components into a manufacturing process with repetitive procedures and resulting cost savings. Entire housing units can be trucked to the site and erected into position. Forty-five years ago, I attended a seminar at MIT on modular construction

The change to off-site and modular construction also includes shifting to robotics. ConXtech is a modular structural framing system with safety potential. Nicolas Mangon, Autodesk VP, stated in ENR that, "this change [to robotics] will ultimately create more jobs. There will be a new group of middle prefabricators that will have those capabilities and reduce the scope of the general contractors." There is no consensus that jobs will be created to offset the loss. We hope that the Autodesk optimism will prevail. Autodesk is a leader in providing software to develop 3D printing, project visualization, and use of artificial intelligence. in the developing construction industry.

OWNERS SUPPORT

OWNER'S REPRESENTATIVE

This would seldom be a different delivery system. A sophisticated owner with a construction staff may designate a lead person as owner's representative or he may be called project manager. An owner without a construction staff may hire a consultant as an owner's representative. The CM as advisor or agent holds some of the same functions; however the CM has shared responsibilities with the architect, contractor, and owner. The CM possibly will have the authority to reject non-conforming work.

CLERK OF THE WORKS

This title is probably obsolete. It has the historical aspect of tradesmen following a project underway in behalf of the owner. The Clerk of the Works responsibility was limited to inspect the work for conformance to plans and established requirements. There was no responsibility to assist in the design phase.

QUALIFIED PERSON (OSHA DEFINITION)

"One who, by possession of a recognized degree, certificate, or professional standing, or who by extensive knowledge, training and experience has successfully demonstrated ability to solve or resolve problem relating to the subject matter, the work, or the project."

A qualified person is required to perform critical inspections under OSHA, B30 Standards and other regulations.

CHAPTER 6
CONSTRUCTION SITE SAFETY

SAFETY PLANNING

Safety planning is the most important item for establishing a construction safety program. The construction operations are controlled by either a prime contractor which is designated a general contractor or a construction manager. The PC/CM/GC is responsible for planning, organizing, monitoring and controlling the construction operations such as means and methods. Job site safety traditionally is the responsibility of the PC/CM/GC. Best practices indicate that the contract documents should assign safety duties to the PC/CM/GC or to an individual, and specifically assign the task of preparing the site safety plan in cooperation with the subcontractors. It should cover all aspects of safety on the specific site including crane safety.

The site specific safety plan may be submitted with bid or prepared after award but before construction. The plan will reflect the hazards, required controls and procedures to integrate the project schedule for any time dependence relationship. Some typical issues to be addressed may be: listing all overhead and underground utilities that could interfere with crane operations, criteria to protect the public from dust, traffic, and noise, specific hoisting equipment inspection, and special procedures to protect the public and users of the facility.

THE SITE SAFETY PLAN

Prepared by the PC/CM/GC prior to start of work, it is assembled with input from subcontractors. This reflects requirements from the contract documents and all phases of safety on the site including crane safety. The site safety plan is considered best practice, required by ANSI A10.33 and A10.38. A10.33 states that "each contractor shall develop, document and implement a site specific Safety and Health plan...."

Multi-Employer Projects: OSHA confines its regulations to the specific employer. ANSI A10.33 addresses the "Safety and Health Program for Multi-Employer Projects." It designates a senior project supervisor who has responsibility for the safety of the entire project. Each prime contractor in turn will have a senior project supervisor.

ASCE Policy 350: The American Society of Civil Engineers (ASCE) Policy 350 is a concise description of the parameters of construction site safety. The Civil Engineering Society is the engineering organization directly involved in construction management and facility design. This policy was first approved in 1989.

The 2019 Policy 350: Safety issues should be addressed for each project on a project-specific basis, starting in project planning and continuing through design and construction. The extent to which a party is expected to contribute to safety on a project is based on the extent to which the party's scope of work and responsibilities affect the safety of the workers and public. Safety roles and responsibilities of each party should be explicitly delineated in the contract documents.

Owners: Owners have the responsibility for assigning project safety oversight and authority to a specific organization(s) or individual(s) on the project. Responsibilities with respect to safety should be assigned to an organization or individual based on the organization or individual's ability to foresee the safety hazards that will be present on the project and to affect the implementation of safety practices/procedures and the outcome of their implementation.

Design Professionals: Design professionals have the responsibility for recognizing that safety and constructability are important considerations when preparing construction plans and specifications.

Prime / General Contractors: Prime/general contractors have the responsibility for control of the overall worksite during construction, and for complying with all applicable safety regulations. Prime/general contractors should proactively manage and maintain the safety of their own employees, be aware of safety programs instituted on site by others, and ensure that all other employers onsite proactively manage and maintain the safety of their employees while on the site.

LANGUAGE ISSUES

If the Hispanic workforce is significant on a construction project, a detailed program shall be developed. In an OSHA "Success Story" for the construction of Dallas/Fort Worth Airport, a mandatory 40-hour safety training program was developed by the GC. Classes were in both English and Spanish. In the Spanish classes, time was assigned to teach students how to say basic construction tools in English. The same instruction was given to the English-speaking students to be able to communicate basic tool names in Spanish. Students were given printed materials to take to the job site along with pocket cards with translation. The Hispanic work force typically will have significant injury rates, but this was reversed with actual rates far below the national average.

The OSHA website is a good resource to review when setting up a job site safety program. There are currently ten outreach courses in Spanish which can be ordered; one is the 10-hour construction safety guide. It is important that a concerted effort be made when training a non-English speaking workforce.

In the 1950s, the most widely used immigrant language in the New York area was Italian. I observed many masons and laborers speaking the idiom. Also, a major and growing portion of the leadership in the building industry was Italian. It is an oversimplification to recognize only the Hispanic language as the result of current immigration. We should expect in the future, more project managers, engineers, designers, future owners and industry leaders will be Spanish-speaking members of the construction workforce.

In the OSHA Final Rule, there are certain conditions when the crane operator can be tested in his or her language for qualifications and certifications. The written materials on the equipment in use must be in that same language (See OSHA Final Rule 1926.1427). An important safety item: the crane lift director must ensure that the communication of the operator with signalmen and riggers is not compromised with language issues.

MANUFACTURERS SAFETY RESPONSIBILITIES FOR CONSTRUCTION EQUIPMENT

ASME B30

The ASME B30 Standard contains provisions that apply to the construction, installation, operation, inspection, testing, maintenance and use of cranes and other lifting and material movement related equipment. Each B30 standard comprises the equipment so designated *(See Chapter 8)*.

The responsibilities of the crane manufacturer are outlined: 1) provide load rating charts for all crane configurations, 2) provide instruction for the proper assembly, disassembly, operation, inspection, and maintenance of the crane.

Unfortunately, there are no uniform operational crane control configurations in the U.S. There are no regulations requiring these standards.

AEM

The Association of Equipment Manufacturers (AEM) is an industry organization that has issued safety manuals for the many types of construction equipment: excavators, aerial devices, rough terrain forklift trucks, backhoe, digger derricks, mobile cranes, etc. The manuals have been issued for the safety of the equipment operations and maintenance. The caveat in each manual forward states, "This manual is not a substitute for the manufacturer's manual. If you do not have a manufacturer's manual for your particular machine, get a replacement manual… Keep this safety manual and the manufacturer's manual with the machine. Read and understand the manufacturer's manual." It is a basic safety principal that the operator must be able to read the manufacturer's manual. OSHA and AEM created an alliance Oct. 1, 2007 for enhanced outreach and communication.

TEN MOST FREQUENTLY CITED STANDARDS BY OSHA

The following is the list of the most frequently cited standards following inspections by federal OSHA in FY 2018. The importance of the list is to give attention to these hazards. It should be a heads-up to both the construction and general industry as to where to focus site safety planning.

1. Fall protection construction.
2. Hazard communication.
3. Scaffolding general requirements construction.
4. Respiratory protection.
5. Control of hazardous energy (lockout/tagout)
6. Ladders, construction.
7. Powered industrial trucks.
8. Fall protection training.
9. Machinery and machine guarding.
10. Eye and face protection.

Falls by far are the main issues of safety. If you analyze the above list, Item 1: Fall Protection, Item 3: Scaffolding Requirements, Item 6: Ladders Construction, and Item 8: Fall Protection Training all represent this issue.

The incorrect set-up of ladders and scaffolding constitute a serious issue. Safety training on ladders must address selecting the weight or type, angle of incline, proper condition and position to secure the feet, and secure the top and tie the top of the ladder. All too often a ladder supplied for one subcontractor is left in place and other workers summarily adopt it for their use. This can cause confusion in tracking responsibility to supply the correct ladder.

A proper scaffold installation also requires a secure and level foundation.

One should use the scaffold parts from the same manufacturer so as to assure proper fit and integrity. Proper handrails are essential and should be installed as the planks are placed in position. Management must be sure roof edges are protected with guardrails and attention is given to roof opening such as skylights and stairwells. The skylight issue is problematic because the responsibility for the protection must be evaluated and assigned. The roofing contractor may be responsible for roof edge protection and the carpentry sub the guard rails or cover for the skylight. The contractor or construction manager must have a system of auditing the jobsite to locate fall hazards prior to work in that area.

EXCAVATION

I am surprised that trenching and general excavation did not make the OSHA top 10 list. In 2017 OSHA was concerned about the number of excavation and trenching accidents: OSHA made a technical presentation to the July 2018 A10 meeting addressing the preventive procedures. There is a 5-foot rule where shoring of a trench is mandated, but the reality is that the soil conditions of all trenches must be evaluated by a "competent person." A procedural question suddenly occurs the moment the excavation reaches the threshold depth. Shoring or a trench box may then be necessary but that may mean an unanticipated delay. Obviously, the depth should have been anticipated.

CHAPTER 7

CRANE SAFETY

CRANES AND DERRICKS USED IN CONSTRUCTION OSHA FINAL RULE

On August 9, 2010 OSHA released the Final Rule, effective November 8, 2010. This is a long-awaited document to update crane safety requirements. It superseded the 1926.550 (1971) OSHA regulation and reflects the technical advances, particularly for hydraulic cranes. The construction industry has continued to update the consensus standards (ANSI B30). However, the 1971 OSHA code was most obsolete. The Final Rule is extensive and has broadened the definition of hoisting equipment. "This standard applies to power operated equipment, when used in construction that can hoist, lower, and horizontally move a suspended load."

SCOPE 1926.1400

The Final Rule applies to cranes used in construction, not in manufacturing. Included are: articulating cranes (when lifting onto construction underway), mobile cranes, and rough terrain cranes. Digger derricks and dedicated drilling rigs are excluded. Multipurpose machines which are also forklifts are considered cranes when they are configured to hoist a load and move a suspended load. Excavators used to hoist a load with a sling are not covered. See 1926.1400 for the complete list.

The hoisting equipment included are greatly expanded from the cranes in the previous standard: 1926.550. If a machine is used in construction with a crane configuration it is likely included in the standards of the Final Rule; however, there is other equipment, such as the common backhoe suspending a load on the jobsite, which is excluded.[1] Construction project managers will be confronted with job risks and accidents from "crane style incidents" from a variety of equipment.

---

1 See section on Commonality of Crane Like Operations, pg. 55

GROUND CONDITIONS 1926.1402

The controlling entity, the general contractor (GC) or the construction manager (CM), has the overall responsibility for construction. The controlling entity must:

1. Ensure that "ground conditions are firm, drained and graded."
2. "Inform the user of equipment and the operator of the locations of hazards beneath the equipment set-up area..."

The OSHA regulations have traditionally emphasized the responsibility of the employer. The Final Rule brings all of the crane regulations closer to the construction industry tradition of the GC and CM responsibility for the entire project.

OPERATOR QUALIFICATIONS & CERTIFICATION 1926.1427

Perhaps the biggest change is the requirement for a third-party certifier of the crane operator. There are four ways that an operator can be qualified or certified:

1. Certified by an accredited crane operator testing organization.
2. Qualification from the employer through an audited program.
3. Qualification by the US Military.
4. Licensing by a state or city government provided it meets the minimum requirements of OSHA.

The Final Rule originally stated that all operators must be qualified or certified by November 10, 2014.

Many in the construction industry have complained about the linkage of certification and qualification, as the employer has traditionally determined if one is qualified to operate the machine to be used. OSHA announced on May 22, 2013 that the compliance date is extended three years to November 10, 2017. This partial reopening of the Final Rule was to address two industry concerns:

1. Certification by capacity—Should other factors such as boom length be tested in addition?
2. Is certification equivalent to qualification?

An OSHA News Release of August 30, 2017 further extended the compliance date to November 10, 2018. In the interim, the employer must train the operator to be compliant to the rule.

QUALIFICATION OF CRANE OPERATORS

On May 21, 2018 OSHA amended the training and certification rule with comments due by June 20, 2018. The pre-existing, or as written standard, allowed operators to be qualified on any crane with the same or lower capacity to that on which they were tested. After resistance from testing agencies, who stated that they did not offer certification by capacity, and training cost concerns, the mandate for rated capacity will now be dropped. This new rule also confirms the requirement that the employer must determine the operator's competency on site. This meets the concern of the many crane owners and employers who wanted to retain this traditional responsibility. An operator cannot simply show up for work with his or her certification as proof of competency. The safety manager or superintendent must evaluate the operator.

An OSHA Trade Release on November 7, 2018 outlined the final interpretation on crane operator certification requirements. The rule now requires employers to train operators as needed to perform crane activities. The rule also requires crane operators to be certified or licensed and receive ongoing training based upon the crane's type and capacity, or type only. The Final Rule on crane certification became effective on February 7, 2019. The evaluation of competency by the owners went into effect on February 7. The industry has made a sigh of relief to finally conclude on this issue. OSHA has yet to issue a definition of a proper evaluation. This will create a push for operator training.

CRANE SAFETY RESPONSIBILITIES

ZONES OF RESPONSIBILITY

This figure has become a popular way to understand crane lifting responsibilities. It was developed early on with the crane committee. The actual originator was Howard Shapiro. It was included in the Crane Safety on Construction Sites Manual No. 93 published in 1998. The operator responsibility is from the hook upward. Rigging responsibility is the hook and lower. The lift director has prime responsibility for the entire lift and must assign the outrigger support to either the rigger or the operator. I was the lead author and chairman of the Crane Safety Committee of the ASCE, a professional organization.

The following responsibilities have been developed in the ASCE Manual No. 93 Crane Safety on Construction Sites:

Rigging Function
Rigging personnel are responsible:
- Under the direction of the lift director.
- Landing the load.
- Verifying the actual weight of the load and communicating same to the operator.
- Verifying the stability of the load, tag lines, load pickup procedures. Signaling by communication with the operator.

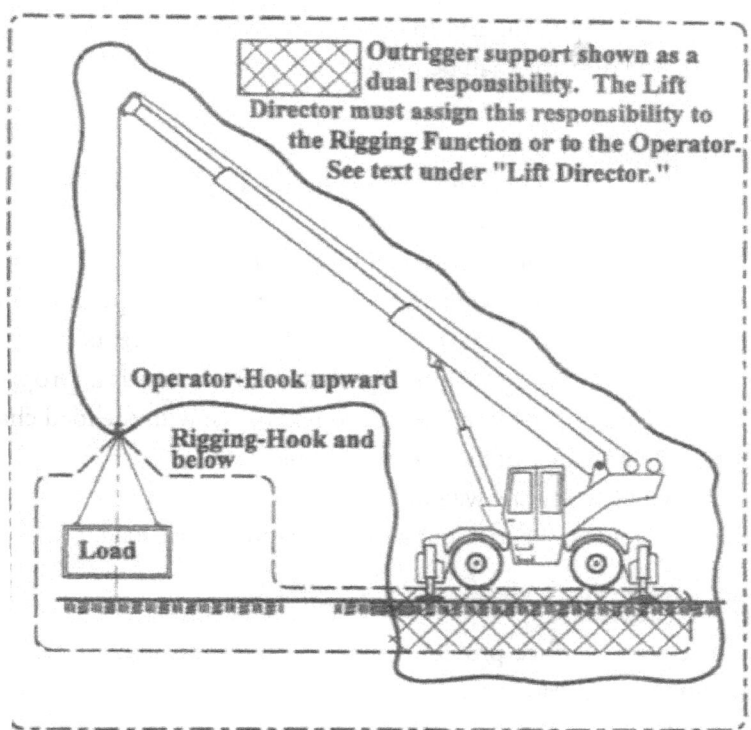

- Rigging the load (attaching) from the bowl of the hook downward.
- Assisting the crane operator in maintaining clearance from obstructions.
- The leader shall ensure that the rigging personnel are properly trained.
- The leader shall survey the site and the path of the load as well as the landing area.

Lift Director
- Assure that the lift plan is current, present in the work area and signed off in accordance with the Crane Safety Plan.
- Assure that the other parties; i.e. riggers, operator, signal persons understand their function in accordance with the lift plan.
- Make a clear assignment of the outrigger duties.
- Assigning/identifying a designated leader of the rigging crew and clearly identifying this leader to all other parties concerned with the lift.
- Assure that a signal person is assigned. Identify the signal person to the operator and all others associated with the lift.
- The director shall be present during a critical lift.

Operator
- All crane movements from the hook upward as well as swing and travel motions.
- The operator may abort the lift at any time.
- Being familiar with the equipment and the operating manual, including load charts and inspection requirements.
- Confirming that the configuration of the crane is appropriate for the load to be lifted and in conformance with the load chart.
- Being aware of the site conditions
- Confirming the weight of the load.
- Knowing the location and destination of the load.

Service Provider
The crane service provider is the party responsible for bringing the crane onto the jobsite and assures:

1. That the erection and dismantling procedures provided by the manufacturer were adhered to.
2. That the inspection prior to the crane operation is performed.
3. That the operator and oiler are properly trained and competent to operate the crane.
4. That the certifications for the crane are in accordance with the crane safety plan and regulatory requirements.

User

The user is an entity that is engaged in rigging or hoisting operations and uses the crane. The user will assign a lift director and shall assure that the rigging crew is qualified.

The ANSI standard ASME B30.5 lists the responsibilities of the crane operator, and the lift director. There are many similarities to the above; however, B30.5 emphasizes the operation of the participants. Two crane operator responsibilities: item (k), "ensuring that all controls are in the off or neutral position and that all personnel are in the clear before energizing the crane or starting the engine." Item (m), "testing the crane function controls that will be used and operating the crane only if those function controls respond properly." I encourage everyone to read the ASME B30.5 consensus standard to better understand the operational responsibilities of the operator, lift director, crane owner, crane user, and site supervisor. The lift director and supervisor may be the same person. The site supervisor would be a higher project manager.

The Crane Safety Responsibility Matrix indicates specific action for various operations. All members of the construction industry and their level of responsibility are indicated. For instance, the prime contractor or CM has the prime (P) responsibility for the crane safety plan and the service provider (SP) as a secondary (S) responsibility. The regulatory agency makes rules (R) for the crane safety plan. Table 3-1, pg. 51 (enclosed) is from the ASCE Crane Safety Manual No. 93. It represents our thinking in the Crane Committee in 1998. There would be variations on these conclusions.

RISK AWARENESS
Crane Overturning:
- Lifting at radius too great for the load.
- Lifting a load too heavy for set-up.
- Failure of crane foundation.
- No cribbing.
- Structural failure.
- Lifting with hoist not vertical.
- Impact forces from too rapid lifting.

Miscellaneous:
- Contact power line.
- Workers not clear of load.
- Two blocking.
- Load shifting.
- Induced electrical charges.

LIFT PLANS

ASCE Crane Safety on Construction Sites Manual 93 of 1998 listed the General Lift Plan, The Production Lift Plan, and the Critical Lift Plan.

GENERAL LIFT PLAN
- Lifts that are neither critical nor production are general.
- List any restrictions because of weather limitations, time of day, or temperature.
- Require that the weight of the load be known.
- Give a description of the rigging equipment.
- Require that a lift director is in charge of each lift.
- Require that a signal person be assigned and clearly identified.

PRODUCTION LIFT PLAN
- Production lifts are repetitive.
- Contain a physical description of the class of items to be lifted. This includes size and shape, weight, and center of gravity.
- Identify the specific arrangement of rigging equipment.
- Identify the specific type and capacity of lifting equipment required.

TABLE 3-1. Crane Safety Responsibility Matrix.

Responsible Organization / Work Performed	Agencies/Agents					Construction			Project[1]		Crane		
	Industry Associations	Professional Societies	Certification (Personnel)	Standards	Regulatory	Service Provider (SP)[2]	Utilizer	Prime Contractor/ Construction Manager (PC/CM)	Architect & Engineer (A&E)	Owner (Public or Private)	Crane Owner	Certifier	Manufacturer
Project													
Contract Document	G	G	G	G	G				A	p			
Crane													
Design	G			G									P
Fabrication	G			G									P
Manuals	G												P
Certification	G			G	R	S					p	A	S
Operation													
Crane Safety Plan						R	S	a	P				C
Transport (On-Site)						R	P						C
Transport (Off-Site)						R	S				P		C
Erection						R	P						C
Use						R	P						C
Dismantling						R	P						C
The Training of:[3]													
Managers	G	G					P	P					G
Supervisors	G	G					P	P					G
Riggers	G	G	a				S	S					G
Operators	G	G	a			S	S	S	S				G

[1] If the owner and A&E are one entity, then the owner has the responsibilities of both.
[2] The SP may be employed by the PC/CM or other utilizer. If the SP is the PC/CM or other utilizer, then SP responsibilities always flow upward to either the PC/CM or other utilizer.
[3] Employees of either the PC/CM or utilizer.

Responsibility Levels
A = Action Agent Primary. The organization that initiates the performance of and may perform the work.
a = Action Agent Secondary. An organization that performs the work and passes the work product to the Action Agent Primary.
G = Guidance. An organization that provides guidelines, manuals, and/or suggestions relating to the "Work Performed."
p = Primary Responsibility. An organization that is responsible for ensuring that certain work is performed.
P = Primary Responsibility plus Primary Action Agent. An organization that is responsible for ensuring that work is performed, as well as being the Action Agent for performing work.
S = Secondary Responsibility. An organization that does not have Primary Responsibility but has a compelling interest in seeing that the work is performed.
C = Sets crane capability. An organization that sets the crane's capability.
R = Makes rules. An organization that makes rules for various crane operations.
Blank = No designated responsibility.

CRITICAL LIFT PLAN
- Any lift utilizing multiple cranes.
- The weight to be lifted compared to the allowable lift.
- The overall risk, difficulty, or complexity of the lift, or toxicity of the product being lifted.
- Critical lifts require individual lift plans.
- Identify the person in charge of the entire lifting operation as the lift director.
- Include a physical identification of the item to be lifted including exact weight, dimensions, location of the center of gravity, and the presence of any hazardous or toxic material;
- Include the identification of the hoisting equipment required by type, rated capacity, boom length, and configuration;
- Include an identification of the required rigging including the capacity of any slings or rigging accessories, below the hook lifting devices, and/or attachment devices. An arrangement drawing may be required;
- Include the utilization of any load indicating devices or load moment indicators that the lift director may require;
- Include a projected path of hoisting and swinging that shows the travel path of the load from the lift-off until final placement;
- Include a hazard analysis of the consequences of failure of the rigging and/or crane during the lift procedure and methods to minimize those exposures;
- Contain an analysis of the capacity of the crane throughout the **entire load path**;
- Include an analysis of weather factors including wind and temperature that may affect the safety of the lift and appropriate restrictions and methods of determining when these limits are approached and/or exceeded;
- Assure that the crane position and orientation are as outlined in the site specific crane safety plan and that the crane location is in an approved area;
- Assign designated signaler(s), and provide for continuous communications. If more than one signaler is required, a "hand-off point" must be defined. If electronic communications are utilized, either redundant systems or a fail-safe lack of communication stop order or procedure must be employed;

- Define the safety quality assurance/control (QA/QC) verifications that are required prior to making the lift. A detailed testing protocol shall be included for each test required;
- Require a meeting involving all participating personnel to be held prior to making a critical lift wherein the plan procedure shall be thoroughly reviewed and any questions or reservations resolved;
- Stipulate that the lift shall not proceed unless the lift director has assured that the crane operator and the designated leader of the rigging crew understand the requirements of the critical lift.

Other standards also address the critical lift:

ASME P30.1- 2014, ASME B30.5, and Specialized Carriers & Rigging Association (SC&RA) Guide to Mobile Crane Safety Management.

ASME P30: The ASME P30.1 includes a *Standard Lift Plan* and a *Critical Lift Plan*.

Standard Lift Plan
- » Plan development: the load center of gravity.
- » Rigging.
- » Site conditions.

Critical Lift Plan
- » Lift Plan development.
- » The load; identify the weight, center of gravity, and dimensions.
- » Load handling equipment: Ensure that the LHE is in compliance.
- » Rigging.
- » Load handling equipment and travel path.
- » Personnel.
- » Site, services and ancillary equipment.
- » Communication system.
- » Site control.
- » Contingency considerations emergency action plan.
- » Pre-lift meeting.

ASME B30.5: ASME B30.5 states under Critical Lift: Certain hoisting or lifting operations are recognized to have increased levels of risk to personnel or property.
- Determined by company policy but may also be determined independently by site supervision, project management, or a qualified person.
- The load being lifted is in excess of a predetermined threshold.
- Lifting of personnel.
- Multi-crane lifts.
- Item being lifted if damaged would be irreplaceable.
- The lifting operation is within boom length of power lines.
- Activities considered by site management.
- Critical Lift Plan: See A-2 for listing.

The Specialized Carriers & Rigging Association (SC&RA): The SC&RA Guide recognizes three lift categories: Critical. Intermediate, and Standard.

Critical Lift Criteria
» Loads over power lines, hazardous process equipment, or an occupied building.
» Crane working at 90 percent or more of rated capacity.
» Load will be at elevations where the ability to achieve control becomes questionable.
» A two or more crane lift.
» On lift matrix value over 15. That is a "certain" probability.

Intermediate Lift Criteria
» Not a critical lift.
» Crane will be working at 75 percent to 90 percent of rated capacity.
» A lift risk matrix of 8 to 15.

Standard Lift Criteria
» Crane will work at 75 percent or less of rated capacity.

For brevity, I did not include all items in describing a critical lift. There are differences in the four above sources. It is important that an owner or construction manager develop their own definition of critical lift which would be unique to their organization.

Critical Lift Plan Documentation
- A plan view drawing which shows the location of the crane in relation to the set point, the pick point and surrounding equipment as well as the load transport route to and from the lift site. It should show radii for lifting and tail-swing clearances.
- An elevation view drawing with all clearances: boom to load, boom to load, boom to structures, rigging to obstructions.
- A rigging drawing with the dimensioned location of the center of gravity.

COMMONALITY OF CRANE LIKE OPERATIONS

The OSHA Regulations Final Rule covers many types of equipment that "can hoist, lower and horizontally move a suspended load." OSHA Subpart 1926.1400 (a) covers the following equipment:

- Articulating cranes (such as knuckle- boom cranes);
- Crawler cranes;
- Floating cranes;
- Cranes on barges;
- Locomotive cranes;
- Mobile cranes (such as wheel-mounted, rough-terrain, all-terrain, commercial truck-mounted, and boom truck cranes);
- Multi-purpose machines when configured to hoist and lower (by means of a winch or hook) and horizontally move a suspended load;
- Industrial cranes (such as carry-deck cranes);
- Dedicated pile drivers;
- Service/mechanic trucks with a hoisting device;
- Crane on a monorail;
- Tower cranes (such as a fixed jib 'hammerhead boom', luffing boom and self erecting);

- Pedestal cranes;
- Portal cranes;
- Overhead and gantry cranes;
- Straddle cranes;
- Sideboom cranes;
- Derricks and variations of such equipment;

MULTI PURPOSE MACHINE:

Multi- purpose machines when configured to hoist and lower (by means of a winch or hook) and horizontally move a suspended load are covered in the Final Rule and considered a crane and must comply with the regulations.

OSHA Subpart 1400 (b) Attachments: "This standard applies to equipment included in para. (a) of this section when used with attachments. Such attachments, whether crane-attached or suspended, include, but are not limited to: hooks, magnets, grapples, clamshell buckets, orange peel buckets, concrete buckets, drag lines, personnel platforms, augers or drills, and pile driving equipment."

The OSHA Final Rule has made a substantial effort to include many types of construction equipment when configured as a crane. Para. (c) of 1926.1400 lists exclusions to the Final Rule. A partial list of the excluded is: power shovels, excavators, wheel loaders, backhoes and loader backhoes, even when used with chains, slings and other rigging to lift suspended loads. Also excluded: automotive wreckers, digger derricks when used for auguring holes for poles in telecommunications, stacker cranes, machinery that hoists by using a come-a-long or chain-fall, dedicated drilling rigs, gin poles when used in erection of communication towers, tree trimming work, articulating/knuckle-boom truck cranes when used to transfer materials to the ground.

OSHA Subpart 1400 (b) Attachments: "This standard applies to equipment included in para. (a) of this section when used with attachments. Such attachments, whether crane-attached or suspended, include, but are not limited to: hooks, magnets, grapples, clamshell buckets, orange peel buckets, concrete buckets, drag lines, personnel platforms, augers or drills, and pile driving equipment."

Chapter 7: Crane Safety | 57

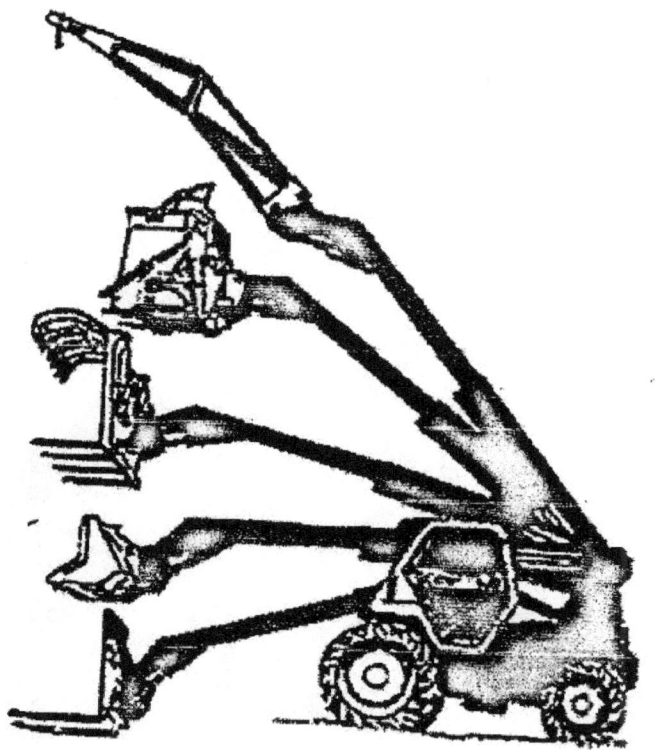

The Multi Purpose Machine

Tower crane at Dartmouth Construction

58 | BEST PRACTICES IN CONSTRUCTION SITE SAFETY

An excavator suspending a load as a crane while following improper crane procedures.

There are many accidents when backhoes and excavators are using a chain-fall suspending a load. This is a typical crane like procedure. Some safety issues: not keeping clear of the load or not using a tag line. OSHA is not specific on using excavation equipment as a crane. One standard: The Association of Equipment Manufacturers (AEM) produces manuals for each specific type of equipment. They are valuable for pre-use check lists. The only crane use mentioned in the excavator safety manual states, "Do not lift or swing a load or attachment over anyone." It also mentions hand signals, but there are no standard hand signals.

To the left is a typical example of an excavator suspending a load as a crane. It shows a precast concrete pedestal swinging into position. There is a worker underneath and actually touching the pedestal. It is a good example of not following proper crane procedures by staying clear of the load and using a tag line. The workers are not wearing hardhats.

Other boom equipment which present possible overturning risks:
- **Concrete Pumps** utilize a long boom which requires outriggers to be in position with emphasis on the supporting strength of the ground below. The Concrete Pump Manufacturers Association (CPMA) has developed a voluntary safety standard.
- **Boom Supported Aerial Work Platforms**: The long boom and reachability of the equipment create a risk in overturning. Training is very important: requirements are found in ANSI/SIA A92.5.
- **Fire Department Ladder Trucks**: The long ladder extensions require the proper application of outrigger supports and in addition following the manufacturers loading instructions. This equipment is vulnerable to overturning. We investigated an overturn situation and determined that it was an operator problem of not setting the outriggers, not a manufacturer issue. The digger derrick is typically used by the utility industry to set poles. If the crane function is used in general construction, outside the utility industry, the OSHA Final Rule and crane regulations govern.

A safety "program" or safety policy would be well advised to train project managers, equipment operators, and workers assigned to such equipment in the basic parameters of lifting operations when using devices that are not called cranes, but in reality are subject to the same dynamics as found in cranes. The OSHA Final Rule has closed the gap by including other types of equipment in the regulations when configured as a crane.

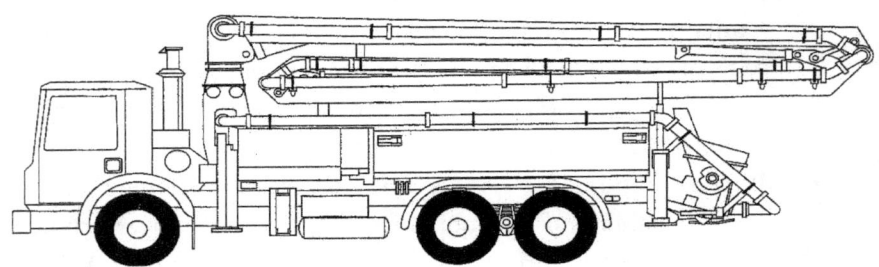

Material Placement System: Truck-Mounted Concrete Pump with Integrated Placing Boom

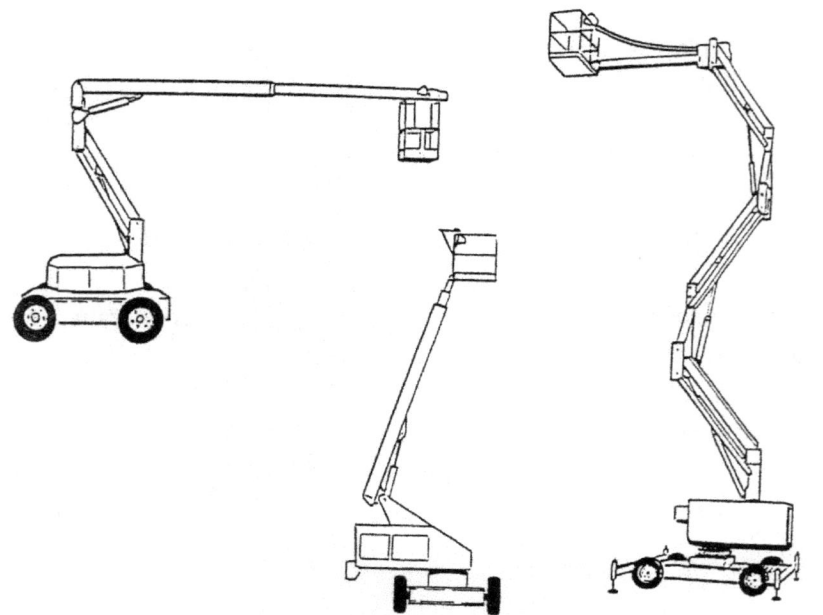

Boom Supported Equipment

OSHA STANDARD HAND SIGNALS FOR CONTROLLING CRANE OPERATIONS

 **STOP** – With arm extended horizontally to the side, palm down, arm is swung back and forth.	 **EMERGENCY STOP** – With both arms extended horizontally to the side, palms down, arms are swung back and forth.	 **HOIST** – With upper arm extended to the side, forearm and index finger pointing straight up, hand and finger make small circles.
 **RAISE BOOM** – With arm extended horizontally to the side, thumb points up with other fingers closed.	 **SWING** – With arm extended horizontally, index finger points in direction that boom is to swing.	 **RETRACT TELESCOPING BOOM** – With hands to the front at waist level, thumbs point at each other with other fingers closed.
 **RAISE THE BOOM AND LOWER THE LOAD** – With arm extended horizontally to the side and thumb pointing up, fingers open and close while load movement is desired.	 **DOG EVERYTHING** – Hands held together at waist level.	 **LOWER** – With arm and index finger pointing down, hand and finger make small circles.
 **LOWER BOOM** – With arm extended horizontally to the side, thumb points down with other fingers closed.	 **EXTEND TELESCOPING BOOM** – With hands to the front at waist level, thumbs point outward with other fingers closed.	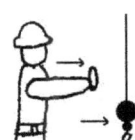 **TRAVEL/TOWER TRAVEL** – With all fingers pointing up, arm is extended horizontally out and back to make a pushing motion in the direction of travel.

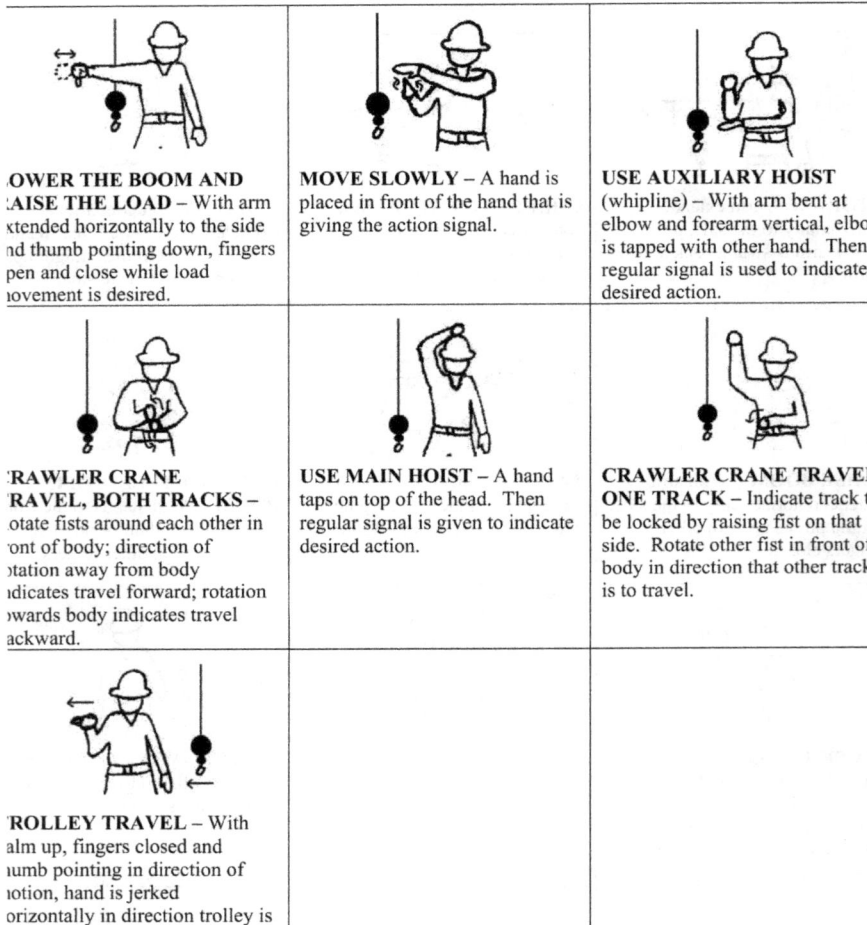

LOWER THE BOOM AND RAISE THE LOAD – With arm extended horizontally to the side and thumb pointing down, fingers open and close while load movement is desired.

MOVE SLOWLY – A hand is placed in front of the hand that is giving the action signal.

USE AUXILIARY HOIST (whipline) – With arm bent at elbow and forearm vertical, elbow is tapped with other hand. Then regular signal is used to indicate desired action.

CRAWLER CRANE TRAVEL, BOTH TRACKS – Rotate fists around each other in front of body; direction of rotation away from body indicates travel forward; rotation towards body indicates travel backward.

USE MAIN HOIST – A hand taps on top of the head. Then regular signal is given to indicate desired action.

CRAWLER CRANE TRAVEL ONE TRACK – Indicate track to be locked by raising fist on that side. Rotate other fist in front of body in direction that other track is to travel.

TROLLEY TRAVEL – With palm up, fingers closed and thumb pointing in direction of motion, hand is jerked horizontally in direction trolley is to travel.

CHAPTER 8
REGULATIONS AND STANDARDS

ANSI ASSP A10 COMMITTEE

This is the Accredited Standards Committee on Safety in Construction and Demolition Operations, A10. There are 47 unique safety standards that serve as a guide to contractors, labor, and equipment manufacturers. The American Society of Safety Professional (ASSP), formerly known as ASSE, is the Secretariat of the ANSI A10 Committee. The use of American Standards is voluntary. They are consensus standards where substantial agreement has been reached by directly and materially affected interests. Consensus requires that all views be considered and that a serious effort be made toward their resolution. Organization representatives belong to all the interest groups: professional societies, contractors, owners, manufacturers, regulatory and governmental agencies. Subcommittees work on the specific standards which are presented to the main committee for a vote by some 75 organizations of interest. The main committee meets twice per year and sub committees meet as required to develop or update a respective standard.

I continued to represent ASCE to the A10 committee. The ASCE representation meets with other society members through a teleconference when a vote is scheduled. This is most valuable as the group has broad and extensive construction experience. When a vote by the full A10 committee fails to attain the necessary approval, the standard is then returned to the originating sub-committee for a rewrite, changes, reconsideration, etc. The resulting standard is current with the industry practices and represents practical safety solutions.

These standards will often serve as a guide to government agencies having jurisdiction over subjects that the A10 Committee has addressed. These standards may be adopted by these agencies and become law.

The A10 standards are voluntary, however they may become mandatory if incorporated in an OSHA standard. A consensus standard can carry considerable weight in a legal forensic case because it represents the industry safety requirements.

Below is a list of existing and proposed standards in the A10 series for safety in construction and demolition.

A10.1 Pre-Project & Pre-Task Safety & Health Planning
A10.2 Safety, Health and Environmental Training (under development)
A10.3 Powder-Actuated Fastening Systems
A10.4 Personnel Hoists and Employee Elevators
A10.5 Material Hoists
A10.6 Demolition Operations
A10.7 Transportation, Storage, Handling, and Use of Commercial Explosives and Blasting Agents
A10.8 Scaffolding
A10.9 Concrete and Masonry Construction
A10.10 Temporary and Portable Space Heating Devices
A10.11 Personnel and Debris Nets
A10.12 Excavation
A10.13 Steel Erection
A10.14 Safety Belts, Harnesses, Lanyards, and Lifelines
A10.15 Dredging
A10.16 Tunnels, Shafts, and Caissons
A10.17 Safe Operating Practices for Hot Mix Asphalt (HMA) Construction
A10.18 Temporary Roof and Floor Holes, Wall Openings, Stairways, and Other Unprotected Edges
A10.19 Pile Installation and Extraction Operations
A10.20 Ceramic Tile, Terrazzo, and Marble Work
A10.21 Safe Construction and Demolition of Wind Generation/Turbine Facilities (under development)
A10.22 Rope-Guided and Non-Guided Workers' Hoists
A10.23 Safety Requirements for the Installation of Drilled Shafts (under development)
A10.24 Roofing – Safety Requirements for Low-Sloped Roofs
A10.25 Sanitation in Construction
A10.26 Emergency Procedures for Construction Sites
A10.27 Hot Mix Asphalt Facilities

A10.28 Work Platforms Suspended from Cranes or Derricks
A10.29 Aerial Platforms in Construction (under development)
A10.31 Digger-Derricks
A10.32 Personal Fall Protection Used in Construction and Demolition Operations
A10.33 Safety and Health Program Requirements for Multi-Employer Projects
A10.34 Public Protection
A10.37 Debris Nets
A10.38 Basic Elements of a Program to Provide a Safe and Healthful Work Environment
A10.39 Construction Safety and Health Audit Program
A10.40 Reduction of Musculoskeletal Problems in Construction
A10.41 Equipment Operator and Supervisor Qualifications and Responsibilities (under development)
A10.42 Rigging Qualifications and Responsibilities in the Construction Industry
A10.43 Confined Spaces in Construction (under development)
A10.44 Lockout/Tagout in Construction
A10.46 Hearing Loss Prevention
A10.47 Highway Construction Safety
A10.48 Communication Tower Erection (under development)
A10.49 Control of Health Hazards (under development)

I attended the A10 Committee meetings of July 10, 2018 and July 16, 2019. There were two areas of current interest:

A10 MEETING, JULY 2018

The A10 sponsored a technical report: A10.100 on "Prevention Through Design." This report is detailed and comprehensive. It investigates solving construction safety problems at the project design phase as well as life cycle issues. There have been many reports on this subject but there still remains a slowness in the construction industry of accepting and implementing the concept. The issues of coordination and liability need to be solved.

A new Fall Protection Standard has been proposed that will involve project planning and providing alternative solutions for fall protection.

The existing standard A10.32 provides information on specific hardware and products will be phased out. No recognition of enhanced digital AI input in the future.

A10 MEETING, JULY 2019 AND JANUARY 2020

The July 2019 meeting established a committee to evaluate AI and current state of the art safety issues. The objective will result in a technical report. I volunteered to be on the committee. AI should now be front and center in the A10 Committee and the construction industry, but it does not yet know how to proceed. It is not an easy turn of direction for construction. The liability issues must be addressed. The A10 Committee is the only organization that can take the lead in this most important task.

AMERICAN SOCIETY OF MECHANICAL ENGINEERS (ASME) B30 COMMITTEE

The B30 Committee has written 30 distinct standards or volumes for cableways, cranes, derricks, hoists, hooks, jacks, and slings under the consensus approval process. These are listed below. Various lifting devices are covered in separate volumes, i.e. B30.3 Tower Cranes, B30.5 Mobile and Locomotive Cranes, B30.6 Derricks, B30.14 Side Boom Tractors, etc.

The B30 standards are often listed in whole or in part for governmental purposes. Each volume may have sections that are designate as mandatory.

The B30.5 Standard covers mobile and locomotive cranes. The B30.5-2014 contains a comprehensive outline of the responsibilities of crane owner, crane user, site supervisor, lift director and crane operator. The standard retains a unique status as a most used and recognized standard. Specific operations include 'holding the load, moving the load, work near electrical transmission lines, signals, etc.

B30.1 Jacks, Hydraulic Gantries
B30.2 Overhead and Gantry Cranes
B30.3 Tower Cranes

B30.4 Portal and Pedestal Cranes
B30.5 Mobile and Locomotive Cranes
B30.6 Derricks
B30.7 Winches
B30.8 Floating Cranes and Derricks
B30.9 Slings
B30.10 Hooks
B30.11 Monorails and Underhung Cranes
B30.12 Handling Loads Suspended from Rotocraft
B30.13 Storage / Retrieval Machines
B30.14 Side Boom Tractors
B30.15 Mobile Hydraulic Cranes (Withdrawn 1982. See B30.5)
B30.16 Overhead Hoists
B30.17 Overhead and Gantry Cranes
B30.18 Stacker Cranes
B30.19 Cableways
B30.20 Below the Hook Lifting Devices
B30.21 Lever Hoists
B30.22 Articulating Boom Cranes
B30.23 Personnel Lifting Systems
B30.24 Container Cranes
B30.25 Scrap and Material Handlers
B30.26 Rigging Hardware
B30.27 Material Placement Systems
B30.28 Balance Lifting Units
B30.29 Self-erecting Tower Cranes
B30.30 Ropes

OTHER STANDARDS

ASME P30.1-2014, Planning for Load Handling Activities augments the ASME B30 standards. P30.1 addresses the planning of all load handling. The ASME B30 standards address the operational issues. It provides details for the Standard Lift Plan and the Critical Lift Plan.

NEW YORK CITY LOCAL LAW 81

NYC adopted Local Law 81 in November 2017. This local law expands the role of the construction superintendent and increases the range of projects where a superintendent is required: all buildings regardless of number of stories (except one to three family homes), new buildings, demolition of a building, vertical or horizontal enlargement, special inspections for underpinning, and special inspections for protection of excavations. The specific responsibilities of the superintendent are addressed such as the daily inspection when active work is underway.

The superintendent must inspect all areas and floors and verify that work is being conducted in accordance with sound practices. He must further make sure that any unsafe condition is corrected.

SITE SAFETY MANAGER

NYC retains the use of a licensed site safety sanager for construction involving 15 stories or more and/or 100,000 square feet or more in area.

NEW YORK CITY LOCAL LAW 196

NYC adopted Local Law 196 in 2017. Beginning March 1, 2018, many building construction workers must have 10 hours of safety training. The worker must show that he or she has taken at least the OSHA 10-hour course within the past five years. By 2019 job sites that have a site safety plan and have a site safety manager or designated superintendent must receive a minimum of 40 hours training. Every worker is to carry a Site Safety Training (SST) card which certifies completion of the training. Contractors are turning to modern technology such as Spot-R by Triax Technology to monitor all workers on site.

BUILDING CODE

The International Building Code: In 2000 the BOCA, ICBO and SBCCI codes were consolidated to form the International Building Code (IBC). It forms the basis for the various state codes including: use and occupancy classification, types of construction, fire resistance- rated construction, means of egress, accessibility, structural design, materials as concrete, masonry, steel, etc.

The building code which is enforced by each municipality or agency iIn New Hampshire is the International Building Code (IBC) with state amendments. In Hanover N.H., ordinance #15 forms a code for the municipality. These codes adopt the Life Safety Code (LSC), NFPA 101 (latest edition) and amendments as adopted by the State of New Hampshire. The current IBC in New Hampshire is from 2009 with amendments. The latest additions of the IBC and LSC is from 2018. If a municipality has no adopted building code, then NFPA 5000 should be used.

NFPA LIFE SAFETY

The National Fire Protection Association (NFPA) is the primary coordinator of life safety regulations. NFPA 101 is the recognized Life Safety Code (LSC). The purpose (art. 1.2) is "... to provide minimum requirements with due regard to function, for the design, operation, and maintenance of buildings and structures for safety to life from fire. Its provisions will also aid life safety in similar emergencies."

NFPA 101 is an occupancy-based code. The following are the initial procedures to determine code requirements (art. 1.1).

Determine occupancy classification, i.e, assembly, educational, health care, etc.
1. Is it a new or existing building?
2. Determine occupancy load: The number of people for the means of egress. If two egress routes are provided, and one is designated unusable, at least half the egress capacity must be available.
3. Determine hazard of contents.
4. Refer to applicable occupancy chapter.

Equivalency: Design alternatives may be adopted by the Authority Having Jurisdiction (AHJ) if convinced it meets the intended level of safety of the code. Equivalency must be demonstrated by appropriate technical documentation. The AHJ is typically the local building inspector or fire marshal.

The various occupancy chapters have both an existing code and new code. This makes the LSC code more useable and practical. The codes are written side by side for direct comparison. An example is the dimension criteria for stairs: existing stairs may have a maximum riser height of 8 in. and a minimum tread depth of 9 in. New stairs currently being built shall have a maximum riser height of 7 in. and a minimum tread depth of 11 in.

The various occupancy chapters:
- Special Structures and High Rise.
- New and Existing Assembly Occupancies.
- New and Existing Educational Occupancies.
- New and Existing Day Care Occupancies.
- New and Existing Health Care Occupancies.
- New and Existing Ambulatory Health Care Occupancies.
- New and Existing Detention and Correctional Occupancies.
- One and Two Family Dwellings.
- Lodging or Rooming Houses.
- New and Existing Hotels and Dormitories.
- New and Existing Apartment Buildings.
- New and Existing Residential Board and Care Occupancies.
- New and Existing Mercantile Occupancies.
- New and Existing Business Occupancies.
- Industrial Occupancies.

Means of Egress: Art. 4.5.3 LSC. Two means of egress, as a minimum, shall be provided in every building or structure. The two means of egress shall be arranged to minimize the possibility that both might be rendered impassable by the same emergency condition. Means of egress shall be maintained free and unobstructed. Means of egress shall be accessible to the extent necessary to ensure reasonable safety for occupants having impaired mobility. Loss of one means of egress requires not less than 50% capacity remaining.

Accessible Means of Egress Art. 7.1.2: A means of egress is considered an accessible means of egress if it meets one of the following criteria:
1) A wheelchair-bound person is able to travel unassisted to a public way. (i.e. ramp-type travel, not stair-type.)
2) A wheelchair-bound person is able to travel unassisted to reach an area of refuge. An area of refuge serves as a staging area from the immediate threatened area and egress to a public way (Art. 3.3.22).

NFPA 1

The fire code has been written as a compendium of all applicable fire codes for use in local fire departments and agencies. It integrates over 50 NFPA codes. Over 100 pages extract from NFPA 101.

ACTIVE CONSTRUCTION

There is a specific relationship to active construction operations. NFPA 101 Article 4.6.10.1 states, "Buildings or portions of buildings shall be permitted to be occupied during construction, repair, alterations or additions only where required means of egress and required fire protection features are in place and continuously maintained for the portion occupied or where alternative life safety measures acceptable to the authority having jurisdiction are in place."

Article NFPA 101 4.6.10.2, "In buildings under construction, adequate escape facilities shall be maintained at all times for use of construction workers. Escape facilities shall consist of doors, walkways, stairs, ramps, fire escapes, ladders, or other approved means or devices."

NFPA 241: This is a standard for safeguarding construction, alteration, and demolition operations.

The NFPA codes directly affect construction site safety.

ADA

The American with Disabilities Act (ADA) first listed iIn the Federal Register Sept. 2010, involves public facilities. The ADA covers 12 categories of public accommodations, stores, restaurants, bars, theaters, hotels, museums, doctor's offices, etc. Grandfathered provisions in building codes do not exempt obligations under ADA. Unlike a building code, the ADA requires barriers to be removed in existing buildings and newly altered or constructed buildings shall be accessible to individuals with disabilities. The ADA emphasizes the building access in the main entrance and the accessible route to the parked vehicle.

An accessible route is a continuous unobstructed path connecting all accessible elements and spaces in a building. This emphasizes all routes such as aisles in a store as well as exterior accessible routes for parking access aisles. The accessibility specifications largely follow ANSI A 117.1. The ADA requires at least one accessible route within the boundary of the site from public transportation, parking, and passenger loading zones. (ART 4.3.2).

ANSI A 117.1

An American National Standard is a consensus document established by the standards committee A117 on Architectural Features and Site Design of Public Buildings and Residential Structures for Persons with Disabilities. It has been made available for adoption by government jurisdictions. Art. 402 Accessible Route, "shall consist of a walking surface with a slope not steeper than 1:20..." The current addition is 2017.

PART III
WHERE WE ARE GOING

CHAPTER 9

DIVERSITY IN CONSTRUCTION

In the 1960s, the unionized construction trades were the center of attention as the construction boom in progress did not offer an increase in jobs to the non-white community. In New York City, 92 percent of the building trades were white (Economic Policy Institute 2017). The union trades through the apprenticeships program provided the opening to the African American community. Today the Black work force is 21.2 percent in NYC union trades and 15.8 percent in non-union work. Minorities are now 55.1 percent of the construction force. (Economic Policy Institute 2017).

In NYC, Hispanic workers are an increasing share of the non-union work force. They are usually recent immigrants, younger, with lower levels of education. The number of Hispanic workers in NYC non-union construction work is at 48.6 percent (Economic Policy Institute 2017). As of 2012, two-thirds of the NYC apprentices were people of color.

The national outlook is quite different from NYC. According to The Bureau of Labor Statistics 2015: the construction work force was 28.5 percent Hispanic/Latino, 9.3 percent female, 6.0 percent black and 1.8 percent Asian. There are a total of 800,000 women employed in construction. There are two sub issues according to OSHA: 1) Personal Protective Equipment (PPE) is often not sized properly for women. 2) Sanitary facilities at the jobsite are found to be inadequate. The Iron Workers has mandated paid maternity leave. There is a National Association of Women in Construction and a Professional Women in Construction organization. Lynelle Cameron, CEO of the Autodesk Foundation, is representative of senior management and a leader in technology to meet the middle east regions sustainability and smart city goals.

Two issues in construction must be addressed: sexual harassment of women and the full integration of African Americans in the workforce. We look for African Americans to join the trades nationally and to become engineers, architects, project managers and owners of construction projects.

CHAPTER 10

PREVENTION THROUGH DESIGN

Prevention Through Design (PtD) might also be designated as Safety by Design. It is an approach which requires the designer, architect, or engineer to "design out" the construction safety risks during the early design development. This approach will lessen the construction reliance on personal protective equipment and on site management.

Some examples of design possibilities to reduce construction hazards:
- Prefabrication of work off site where production controls are enhanced.
- Design early installation of anchorage points for leading edge work.
- Bending the top of reinforcing steel dowels to decrease exposure to impalement.
- Design erector friendly steel column connections to enhance fall protection.
- Relocate a light fixture that will eliminate the need of a ladder or scaffold.
- Relocate hard to reach valves to an accessible location will make it easier to install.
- Design the height of a parapet wall on flat roofs to 42 inches will provide passive fall protection.

PtD has been required in Europe since the 1990's. The National Institute for Occupational Safety and Health (NIOSH) has directly advocated PtD. The American Society of Safety Professionals (ASSP) has issued the Technical Report, Prevention Through Design, ASSP TR-A10.100. "A Life Cycle Approach to Safety and Health in the Construction Industry."

PtD addresses the building life cycle which includes construction, its use and future decommissioning.

With PtD, construction hazards and risks can be identified and addressed during the design process. There is a fear that designers that use PtD will be subject to lawsuits when there is a job site injury. It is not the intention of PtD that designers will have a responsibility to inspect construction work or have involvement with the contractors "means and methods." There is an historical "firewall" between the design profession and the contractor. This is a carryover from the traditional design/contractor model where the construction contract would go out to bid following the completion of the contract documents. This has been recognized in the AIA and Engineers Joint Contract Documents (EJCDC).

Designers need to recognize their responsibilities for safety in the design process. One would think that the PtD concept is a win-win situation. The ASCE is a professional organization that represents both designers and construction firms. I was involved in the change that ASCE went through to recognize the safety responsibilities of designers. There continues to be resistance by the lawyers for design only firms. These are A&E firms that continue to retain the "firewall" by separation from the construction contract. Currently the design-build and construction management delivery systems have integrated the constructor with the designer. That means there is a break through the "firewall" as to constructability but that does not necessarily mean that there is PtD.

A design firm with a contract including PtD may have an inspection of the work function to determine if the work completed was in accordance with the plans and specifications.

Often this assignment gives the designer the responsibility to "stop the work" if there is a problem which might include safety. A plaintiff in an injury case will argue that the designer has a safety responsibility that is inherent in the "stop the work" even if there is a designation in the contract of non-responsibility for site safety or means and method.

The plaintiff can also argue that the PtD by itself means that the designer should have foreseen the hazard that created the condition that was involved with the accident.

CHAPTER 11

THE NEW TECHNOLOGY: AI AND THE DIGITIZED WORLD

This portion of the chapter is out of date.
It was out of date the day it was written.
AI, AR, and VR are developing fast.

Engineering and construction is rapidly starting a new era: one where Virtual Reality (VR) and Augmented Reality (AR) will influence our projects and will have a major impact on construction safety. I wish that I were just starting my career so that I could participate and enjoy this new technology.

VR uses computer programming developed for the game design industry. This software creates the simulation of a real condition or environment. The user feels that he is actively participating in the projected environment. Pilots are being trained in flight simulators using VR. There are some applications already in use in construction equipment operator training.

AR uses a computer-generated overlay of a real or projected condition. This will enable designers, owners and contractors to address problems that arise with an ongoing project. These parties can don a headset and take a virtual tour of the project as originally designed and to evaluate problems of design questions and in shop drawing coordination. After a solution is adopted, the parties can observe what it will look like.

HOW WILL AR CHANGE CONSTRUCTION SAFETY?

Training of construction workers will be enhanced by being able to show the site in different future conditions. Hazards can be readily identified. We will be able to "see" the site. VR is being used for training pilots in simulators. Training of equipment and crane operators will be able to visualize the site with its limiting conditions: i.e. general public safety, overhead wires, unsafe ground conditions, etc. Training tutorials with a picture or physical portrayal of the safety challenges will aid understanding of the course material. Safety programs, revised drawings, safety alerts, etc. can be readily distributed to parties at multiple locations in the country with wi-fi coverage.

Tradesmen with AR glasses will be able to determine the thickness of the concrete pour, thickness of pavement, and check material for conformance to specifications.

The liability and risk could be problematic. Our litigious industry will have to adopt. New parameters and lines of responsibilities will have to be developed. Who is responsible when a robot crane operator drops a load on the adjacent building?

According to commentary on **Innovation 2050** by Balfour Beatty, we will have construction sites with few humans by 2050. Robots will perform the physical work. Project managers can then operate many projects using 3D and 4D visualization. Drones will constantly survey the project providing updates on progress and giving instructions to the robotic work force.

Civil Engineering Magazine (Jan 2018) contained an article on TyBot, a rebar tying system that is equivalent to a team of six to eight workers on a concrete bridge deck. This was produced by Brayman Construction Corp. using artificial intelligence and vision sensors. Tybot can work constantly with only one actual supervisor.

REDPOINT POSITIONING SAFETY VESTS

This is a GPS system that has proven itself as a construction safety aid. A hazardous area can be plotted on a map or drawing and intergraded to a GPS designation. When the wearer of the vest enters the area, it receives an alarm both visually and audibly. The worker is identified, and a record of the entry is maintained. This helps identify the repeat violators. The Redpoint system can also be used to determine if the appropriate crew is actually working at the proper location on the job site and historical records of job progress are recorded.

THE 2020 COVID-19 PANDEMIC

The construction industry now realizes that it has a system to help combat the Pandemic with GPS positioning technology. The IOT system by Triax Technology has a wearable device that can attach to a hardhat that provides social distancing alerts now mandated in many states (keep workers six to ten feet apart). It is also used for contact tracing after a worker is diagnosed with COVID-19.

Virtual Reality and Augmented Reality are helping create a future that is without the typical computer monitor. The Samsung headset called Monitorless allows a user to actively stream content from a computer to the headset. It can be identical to a desktop experience: create Word documents and search the web as well as work on the immediate job at hand. Microsoft HoloLens is another system that allows the user to work untethered to a computer. You can take the work with you.

AI can recognize patterns and process data far more accurately and efficiently than humans. It is particularly valuable in the early design process. It can check for errors. It is machine intelligence.

"Generative Design" tasks a computer with a complex task. Each solution is fed back into the computer to augment the results. Autodesk has developed Project Dreamcatcher and its Generative Design part of its Fusion suite. Algorithms can compare large quantities of data and make corrections that a person cannot accomplish. Autodesk BIM 360 uses AI to analyze projects for safety issues. With AI there is the opportunity to review data at a speed that humans cannot. Imagine that everyone on the project team can call in and obtain a current risk assessment. Project algorithms can review the files and identify areas of risk.

I listened to the webinar of the AI presentation at the ENR San Francisco Forum. A direct question to the presenter: What background must a Project Engineer have to use AI? The reply: A solid background in computer programming. My take is that we need computer skills to develop AI algorithms, but the AI use will be available for all. We need to take advantage of this digital age so that it can lead us to the hazardous locations daily on our jobsites. Some papers show artificial medical radiologists outperforming the ones in white coats. Other papers still put humans ahead.

Autodesk CEO Andrew Anagnost (Nov. 2018 Future Tech show Las Vegas) predicted that in 10 years, construction workflows will be much closer to manufacturing efficiency. He described the new partnership between Autodesk and Unity, "integrates Unity's immersive visualization engine into Autodesk design products, BIM 360 cloud sharing platform and modeling tool, Revit."

At the 2019 Auto-desk University (Future Tech), Andrew Anagnost stated, "Auto-desk will focus on how to better integrate its software with the workflow of on-site robotics as well as pre-fabrication and modular construction."

Nicolas Mangon, Auto-desk VP, said "the typical general contractor today does not have a factory, the theory we are working from is there will be a new group of middle fabricators that will have those capabilities and reduce the scope of the general contractor." The question (2019) relates to the competition between China and the United States on the development and implementation on AI. Has the center of gravity shifted to China? The US has been at the forefront of AI discovery, innovation, and research. China however has shown an ability to take a new breakthrough, then develop and subsidize many tech companies. The conclusion may be that the need for technical improvements would favor the US, but progress on implementation would favor China.

The VR/AR push in China has top level backing. President Xi Jinping speaks of its importance, and the central government's current Five Year Plan includes virtual reality as a focus area of economic growth. In concert with this, a host of government related and supported initiatives have been launched at levels from the national to the local.

The Kiplinger Letter December 2018 has projected that the fastest growing industry over the next five years is health care. Telemedicine, where doctors will monitor patients remotely, will improve health care with the shortage of medical professionals. 5G cellular service will move data up to 100 times faster than the 4G networks. This will have widespread impact on hardware sellers and internet providers. Other industries to watch: drones and driverless cars.

AGI AND SUPERINTELLIGENCE

Kai-Fu Lee was the president of Google China. In his book, AI Super-Powers, Mr. Lee said he believes that there are many decades, if not centuries, for full AGI to develop. The problem ahead is the crisis of jobs and inequality. A greater divide between the haves and have nots? There will be productivity gains but there will also be job layoffs AI will exacerbate global economic inequality. He has designated Risk of Replacement for AI:

Cognitive Labor and Physical Labor. Plumbers and construction represent "slow creep," i.e. vulnerable over time. A physical therapist represents a safe zone. Mr. Lee sees both blue collar and white collar vulnerability to job losses following the rapid advances of AI. He is more pessimistic than many prognosticators on AI. Mr. Lee predicts that "we will technically be able to automate 40 to 50 percent of all jobs within fifteen years."

DEFINITIONS USED IN THIS CHAPTER

VR (Virtual Reality): "An experience that requires a headset to completely replace a user's surrounding view with a simulated immersive and interactive virtual environment." (re: Fink's Meteverse)

AR (Augmented Reality): "Overlaying or mixing simulated digital imagery with the real world as seen through a camera and on a screen. Graphics can interact with real surroundings." (re: Fink's Metaverse)

AI (Artificial Intelligence): "The theory and development of computer systems able to perform tasks that normally require human intelligence, such as visual perception, speech recognition, decision making, and translation between languages." (re: Fink's Metaverse)

AGI (Artificial General Intelligence): Thinking machines with the ability to perform any intellectual task that a human can and much more (AI Super-Powers Kai-Fu Lee).

DEMYSTIFYING AI FOR CONSTRUCTION

Autodesk published a report in 2019 called "Demystifying AI for Construction." This had an immediate appeal to me as I have been trying to understand how AI will help the field of construction site safety. How do I relate the predictive analysis that AI will bring to us through our data input to benefit safety on the jobsite? Autodesk presented Seven Big Ideas, which are condensed below: the subset of AI referred to as machine learning is a specific statistical approach that involves learning by identifying patterns in data sets and modifying the algorithms to achieve better results over time.

IDEA #1
AI Systems Reduce Errors and Expose Insights.

AI systems provide value by identifying patterns and exposing relationships that are nonintuitive, or even counter intuitive, based on data. AI supercharges a company's ability to track progress and get actionable intelligence in real time. The key to exposing insights is to build business systems that effectively capture data that is critical to understanding and improving business performance.

IDEA #2
Learning Happens Most Effectively in Structured Data Platforms.

Standardizing how data is captured and tracked across an organization is effectively step one of the journey toward data analysis excellence. Improving data capture and tracking in a structured environment helps business create a strong foundation that will allow them to quickly derive business value from new technology.

IDEA #3
Human/Machine Collaboration is the Best of Both Worlds.

Machines are better at data processing, while humans are better at generalization. Machines are better at brute strength and rapid motion, while humans excel at adapting to unstructured physical environments. Machines are better at identifying patterns, while humans are better at understanding business implications and executing a strategic plan. These digital collaborations will dramatically increase an individual's capacity to generate value in the trailer or on the jobsite and will support more proactive decision making.

IDEA #4
The Future of Work Will Be Task Automation, Not Job Replacement.

Most jobs in construction involve many disparate, separate tasks, each one requiring a different but related skillset. It is these specific tasks that will be streamlined, optimized, or even automated by AI systems. Automation will increase a human's capacity; fewer workers will be needed to provide the same value.

IDEA #5
AI and Robotics Have Different Development Trajectories.

Automation of tasks is different than directly replacing human jobs, and the robotic construction jobsite is a long way off. Construction has a systemic challenge in that each unique jobsite is a highly unstructured physical space that is rapidly changing. This is a challenging environment for robotics applications.

IDEA #6
AI Applications Will Be Developed Based on Business Value.

When thinking about the implications of AI, construction executives should think in terms of business models—what problems yield a big payoff when solved. The payoff could be in terms of technical excellence, sustainable competitive advantage, stable and scalable profit, or many others.

IDEA #7
The Opportunity is to Increase Capacity; The Challenge is How to Transition.

AI systems will reduce errors and expose insights that will allow the construction industry to increase its value per employee and its effectiveness in project delivery across the project lifecycle. In summary, AI systems will help to increase the capacity of the construction industry to deliver projects sustainably and efficiently. However, the Building Information Modeling (BIM) transformation of the past decade or so has demonstrated that cultural challenges are often just as formidable as technological ones.

PREDICTIVE ANALYTICS

Predictive analytics has been defined in a white paper by a strtegic council as outputs from a model providing insight and answering the question "what will happen?"

My question is, "How will we modify our construction safety standards to incorporate the advantage of AI and predictive analytics?" The white paper states that predictive results are different from the values we are used to seeing in reports because they are outputs from predictive models. You should treat them as insights to be used to enhance decision making but not to make the decision. Preventing incidents is an all hands on deck activity. To that end, sharing the predictive results helps get everyone on the same page working together. The white paper concludes that construction can join other industries and use this powerful analytical approach to reduce risk and improve decision making.

How will AI help? Falls in construction is no 1 on the OSHA list of ten most cited standards. The ANSI/ASSE A10.18 Safety Requirements for Temporary Roof and Floor Holes and Other Unprotected Edges in Construction directly addresses this issue. The standard is simple: guardrail systems, personal fall arrest systems, or safety net systems shall be used at unprotected edges... six or more feet above an adjacent floor or ground level. This could not be more simplistic. Why are we having so many fall accidents and OSHA citations? It is so straight forward. I do not have any experience with predictive analytics, but I am a member of the A10 committee representing ASCE. If the predictive model can be coordinated with the project schedule, then the model could flag a hazardous condition, say when a floor level is poured before guardrails are installed. Then, every subcontractor and responsible manager on the job can be instantly on the same page.

CONCLUSION

There is so much potential to be gained. We are not there yet. Construction managers, project managers, and superintendants need to be educated in AI. This is our challenge.

INDEX

1926.550 regulation, 6, 44
1926.1400 regulation, 44, 55, 56,
    Subpart (a), 55
    Subpart (b), 56
3D printing, 36
AAA. *See* American Arbitration
    Association
absolute standard, 7
action plan, 18, 53
ADR. *See* Alternative Dispute
    Resolution
AEM. *See* Association of Equipment
    Manufacturers
aerial lifts, 4
African American, 29, 75
AGC. *See* Associated General Contractors of America
AI. *See* artificial intelligence
AI Super-Powers, 81-83
AIA. *See* American Institute of
    Architects
AIA A132, 35
AIA B132, 35
AIA C132, 35
Almy, Dr. Tom, 25, 30
Alterman, Philip J., 21
alternative dispute resolution, 9
American Arbitration Association, 9
American Institute of Architects, 7, 34
American Society of Civil Engineers, 4, 20, 21, 34, 39, 49, 50, 63, 77, 85
American Society of Mechanical Engineers, 20, 21, 41, 49, 53, 54, 66, 67
American Society of Safety Professionals, 76
Anagnost, Andrew, 80, 81
ANSI A10, 21, 43, 63-66, 85
ANSI A10.18, 64, 85
ANSI A10.38, 39, 65
ANSI A10.38, 65
ANSI A10.100, 65, 76
ANSI ASME B30, 20, 21, 37, 41, 44, 66, 67,
ANSI ASME B30.4, 21, 67
ANSI ASME B30.5, 20, 21, 49, 53, 54, 66, 67
ANSI/SIA A92.5, 59
AR, *See* augmented reality
arbitration, 9, 14, 17
arbitration hearings, 17
architect, ii, 7, 24, 33, 34, 35, 37, 76
Argentia, Newfoundland, 22, 30
artificial intelligence, i, 36, 66, 78-85
asbestos, 3
ASCE, *See* American Society of Civil
    Engineers
ASCE Policy, 39
Asian, 75
ASME. *See* American Society of
    Mechanical Engineers
ASME P30, 53
ASME P30.1, 53, 67
Associated General Contractors of
    America, 7, 34
Association of Equipment Manufacturers, 41, 58
ASSP. *See* American Society of Safety
    Professionals

Augmented Reality, 78-82
Autodesk, 36, 75, 80-83
Autodesk BIM 360, 80, 81
Autodesk University, 81
Beatty, Balfour, 79
Bellevue Hospital, 25, 26, 30
Bellinzoni v. Birgir Seland, 12
Birmingham, Alabama, 23
Black, 23, 24, 75
blasting, 7, 10, 64
concrete pumps, 59, 60
Brayman Construction Corp., 79
bridge safety inspection, 5
Bridgeport, Connecticut, 5
Bronx, New York, 14, 15
Brooklyn Bridge, 1
Brown, Wes, 29
building code, 15, 68, 69, 71
Bureau of Labor Statistics, 75
Burkart, Matthew J., 21
Cameron, Lynelle, 75
cancer causing substances, 4
carcinogens standards, 4
Carter, President, 4
Cavanaugh, 13, 14
Cavanaugh v. Township of Montclair, 13
CDAC. *See* Cranes and Derricks Advisory Committee
certification, 11, 45, 46
Certification 1926.1427, 40, 45
Chappaqua New York, 26, 27
Chiarelli v. 128 Eighth Ave., 12
China, 81
Civil Engineer Corps, 22, 28, 29
Civil Engineering Magazine, 79
Civil Engineering Society, 39

civil rights, 23, 24
Civil Rights Act, 24
Clerk of the Works, 37
CM. *See* construction managment
code, 7, 12, 13, 15, 16, 20, 27, 44, 68
collapse, 3-6, 12, 13, 20, 28
Common Law, 7
communication, i, ii, 5, 15, 40-42, 47, 52, 53, 56,
computer assisted design, 4
computer technology, 4
concrete, 1, 23, 59, 60, 64, 68, 79
Concrete Pump Manufacturers Association, 59
Connor, Bull, 23
construction management, 9, 18, 27, 34, 39, 77,
construction manager, i, ii, 16, 27, 35, 38, 42, 45, 55, 85
construction quality, 10
construction safety, i, 1, 3, 4, 10, 38, 40, 65, 76, 78, 79, 85
Construction Safety Standards, 4, 85
Construction Scaffold Safety Standard, 6
construction site, i, 2-6, 20, 39, 46, 47, 50, 64, 71, 79, 82
Contract Law, 12
contractor, i, ii, 7, 8, 12-14, 16, 19, 21-23, 25, 28, 29, 33-39, 42, 45, 49, 63, 68, 77, 78, 81, 85
ConXtech, 36
cooling tower, 4
Cornell Medical School, 25, 30
COVID-19, 79, 80
CPMA. *See* Concrete Pump Manufacturers Association

crane operator, 21, 28, 40, 45, 46, 48, 49, 53, 66, 78, 79,
crane safety, ii, 4, 20, 21, 38, 44, 46, 47, 49, 50, 53
Crane Safety Committee, 20, 21, 47
Crane Safety Plan, ii, 48, 49, 52,
Crane Safety Responsibility Matrix, 49
cranes.
    all-terrain, 55
    articulated booms, 20
    articulating cranes, 44, 55
    boom truck, 20, 55, 56
    carry-deck, 55
    commercial truck-mounted, 55
    crawler, 20, 55
    fixed jib, 55,
    floating, 55, 67
    gantry, 56, 66, 67
    hammerhead boom, 55
    industrial, 55
    lattice type booms, 20
    locomotive, 55, 66, 67
    luffing boom, 55
    mobile, 21, 41, 44, 53, 55, 66, 67
    outriggers, 11, 59
    overhead, 56, 66, 67, 79
    pedestal, 21, 56, 67,
    portal, 21, 56, 67
    riggers, 21, 40, 47, 48
    rough terrain cranes, 44, 55,
    self erecting, 55, 67
    sideboom, 56
    standing tower cranes, 6
    straddle, 56
    telescoping booms, 13, 20
    tower, 6, 20, 55, 57, 66, 67
    wheel-mounted, 55

critical lift plan, 50, 52-55, 67
Cuomo, Governor, 27
Dallas/Fort Worth Airport, 40
Dartmouth College, 22, 25, 28, 57
deaths, 1-3
dedicated drilling rigs, 44, 66
demolition, 6, 10, 11, 12, 63-65, 68, 71
depositions, 8, 11, 15
derricks, 1, 6, 20, 44, 56, 59, 65-67
Derzon, Bob, 25
design-bid-build, 33, 35
discriminatory hiring, 24
Dispute Review Board, 9
DRB. *See* Dispute Review Board
dunnage, 14
Eisenhower Hall, 26
EJCD. *See* Engineers Joint Contract Documents
elevated walkways, 4
Empire State Building, 2
Engineering News Record, 29, 36, 80
engineers, ii, 4, 12, 17-19, 21, 23, 29, 33, 34, 40, 66, 76, 80
Engineers Joint Contract Documents, 77
Engineers Joint Council, 7, 34
ENR. *See Engineering News Record*
Erie Canal, 1, 3
excavation, 1, 6, 26, 43, 58, 64
Excavation and Trenching Operations Standard, 6, 43
Fair, Harlan W., 21, 26, 27, 29, 34
falls, 1, 6, 10, 12, 13, 15, 23, 28, 42, 65, 76, 85
Fall protection, 42
Fall Protection Standards, 6, 65
Federal Compensation Act, 2

Federal General Services Administration, 34
Final Rule, i, 6, 21, 40, 44-46, 55, 56, 59
    Sec 1926.1427, 45
    Sec 1926.1432, 21
    Subpart 1400 (b), 56
fire department ladder trucks, 99
five-foot rule, 10
Flood v. City of New York, 12
Floyd Bennett Field, New York, 29
Focht, John A., 20
forensic engineering, 9
Freedom Riders, 3
friction systems, 20
Future Tech, 80, 81
Gallipolis, Ohio, 3
Galuso, Patrick E., 21
GC. *See* general contractor
general contractor, ii, 12, 33-35, 38, 40, 45, 81
general lift plan, 50
generative design, 80
Golden Gate Bridge, 3
Gonzalez v. Anglebrook Limited, 12
Google, 81
Gradall, 13
Greensboro, North Carolina, 24
Greenwich, Connecticut, 5
Gregory, Katherine, 28
Ground-Fault Circuit Interrupter Standard, 5
ground-fault circuit protection, 5
guaranteed maximum price, 27, 35
guardrails, 6, 42, 85
Guide to Mobile Crane Safety Management, 53

Guy F. Atkinson Co., 21
H. Fair Associates, 21, 26, 27
Hard Rock Hotel, 6
hardhats, i, 2, 3, 23, 59
Harkness Medical Research Building, 25
Hartford Civic Center, 4
Hazard Communication Standard, 8
hazardous energy, 5, 42
Health and Hospital Corp, 25-27
HHC. *See* Health and Hospital Corp
Hispanic, i, 23, 40, 75
hot tar, 10, 14, 15
Hyatt Regency, 4
hydraulic clutches, 20
I-95, 5
illiterate, 15
immigrant, 15, 40
immigration community, i
Indianapolis, Indiana, 27
Ingalls Iron, 23
Innovation 2050, 79
IOT system, 79
Iron Workers, 75
Italian, 40
jack hammers, 11
Jacobi Medical Center, 14
James Jones v. Edgewater Park, 15
job site safety, ii, 25, 38, 40
jobsite personnel, i
Johnson, Phillip, 24, 25
Johnson, President, 24
Jones, J.A., 15, 27
Kansas City, Missouri, 4
Kaplan, Joseph, 21
King, Martin Luther, 24
Kiplinger Letter, 81

Kips Bay, 25
L'Ambiance Plaza Collapse, 5
labor law 12, 13
ladders, 10, 12, 13, 42, 59, 76
languages, ii, 82
lateral displacement, 5
Latino, 75
Lee, Kai-Fu, 81, 82
Lentini v. Tishman, Crimmins, 13
lift director, 11, 21, 40, 47-50, 52, 53, 66
lift slab, 5
load rating charts, 41
Lockout Standard, 5
Los Angeles, California, 29
mandate, 46
Mangon, Nicolas, 36, 81
Manhattan, New York, 12-14
manholes, 6
Mansion, The, 15
Manuel Perez v. City of New York, 14, 15
March on Washington, 24
Massachusetts, 1
material safety data sheet, 5
maternity leave, 75
McCoy v. MTA, 13
mediation, 5, 9
Mexican, 15
Mianus River Bridge, 5
Microsoft HoloLens, 80
miners, 1
mining, 1
minorities, 75
MIT, 36
modular, 28, 36, 81
monitorless, 80

Montclair, New Jersey, 13
multi-purpose machines, 55
multi-story atrium, 4
NAFE. See National Academy of Forensic Engineers
Nash, William R., 21
National Academy of Forensic Engineers, 17, 19
National Association of Women in Construction, 75
National Historic Register, 27
National Institute for Occupational Safety and Health, 76
National Safety Council, 2, 18
National Transportation Safety Board, 5
Naval Academy, 29
Naval Facilities Engineering Command, 21, 29
NAVFAC. See Naval Facilities Engineering Command
Navy, 28-30
Navy Civil Engineer Corps, 22
Navy Civil Engineer Corps negligence standard, 7
NCEC. See Navy Civil Engineer Corps negligence standard
New Orleans Hotel Collapse, 6
New Orleans, Louisiana, 6, 22
New York, 2, 9, 12, 14, 15, 17, 23-25, 27-29, 40
New York City, 15, 17, 26, 68, 75
New York Dormitory Authority, 14
New York Hospital, 25, 30
New York Industrial Code, 7, 13
New York State Court of Claims, 18
New York State Scaffold Law, 7, 12

New York World's Fair. *See* World's Fair
NIOSH. *See* National Institute for Occupational Safety and Health
Nixon, President, 3
non-English speaking, 40
NY Manhattan Bridge, 12
NYC Department of Hospitals. *See* Health and Hospitals Corp
Occupational Safety and Health Act, 6
Occupational Safety and Health Administration. *See* OSHA
Occupational Safety and Health Review Commission, 3
Office of Workers' Compensation, 2
Oklahoma City, Oklahoma, 27
OSHA, i, ii, 1, 3, 4-6, 13, 20, 21, 37, 39-41, 46, 55, 56, 58, 59, 61, 63, 68, 75, 85
    OSHA Coverage for Federal Workers, 4
    OSHA Final Rule. *See* final rule
    OSHA Standards, 3
    OSHA State Plans, 4
    OSHA Training and Education Grants, 4
owner's representative. See project manager
pandemic, 16, 79
Park Avenue, 13, 14
Patterson, Floyd, 23
PC, See prime contractor
Pelham Manor, New York, 27
personal protective equipment, 6, 75, 76
pile drivers, 55

Point Pleasant, West Virginia, 3
Policy for Crane Safety, 20
post exchange, 26
Powell v. City of New York, 14
PPE. *See* personal protective equipment
prefabricated, 2, 24
Prevention Through Design, 65, 76
production and inspection, 8
production lift plan, 50
Professional Women in Construction, 75
Project Dreamcatcher, 80
project manager, 27, 37, 40, 44, 47, 59, 79, 85
protective gear, i
PtD. *See* prevention through design
QA. *See* quality assurance
QC. *See* quality control
quality assurance, 53
RA. *See* rigging association
railroad, 1
Redpoint system, 79
regulatory commissions, 1
Respiratory protection, 42
Rigging Association, 53, 54
Right to Know Regulations. *See* Hazard Communication Standard
Robinson, Jackie, 23
robotics, 36, 81, 84
Roebling, John, 1
roof parapets, 15
roofing, 10, 14, 15, 42, 64
Rusi v. Park, 15
safe place to work statute, 8
safety harnesses, 6
safety lines, 3

safety nets, 3
Safety planning, 38, 42
safety violations, 16
Sale, Dwight B., 21
San Francisco, 20, 80
SC. See specialized carriers
scaffolding, 4, 6, 7, 10, 12, 14, 23-25, 42, 64, 76,
Seabee, 22, 29
segregation, 24
service provider, 48, 49
Shapiro, Howard I., 21, 46
Shea Stadium, 26
side slope, 10
signage, 11
signalmen, 40
Silver Bridge, 3
single steps, 10
site safety plan, ii, 38, 68,
skylight, 10, 42
slip form technology, 23
SP. See service provider
space-frame design, 4
Spanish, i, 15, 40
Speaking Out, 29
specialized carriers, 53, 54
stairwells, 10, 42
standard lift plan, 53, 67
standard of care, 8
State of California Highways, 29
State of Connecticut, 5
Statutory Law, 7
steel erection standard, 6
Strauss, Joseph, 3
street traffic controls, 11
subcontractor, ii, 23, 25, 33, 38, 42, 85
supplementary conditions, 7

Susan Harwood Grants. See OSHA Training and Education Grants
suspended walkways, 5
suspension chain, 3
tag out, 11
tagout standard, 5
taglines, i, 13
Tappan Zee, 27, 28
telehandler, 13
telemedicine, 81
Thayer School of Engineering, 22, 28-30
Thompson Starrett Construction Company, 23, 25
training, i, ii, 4, 5, 11, 12, 14-16, 22, 29, 37, 40, 42, 46, 59, 64, 68, 78, 79
training documents, i
transit, 29
trench guard, 10
trenching, 6, 10, 43
Triax Technology, 68, 80
Turner Construction Corp, 25, 29
TyBot, 79
U.S. Department of Labor, 2
Unity, 80
Vals v. Lombardi, 13
Vermont, 28
Virtual Reality, 78, 80-82
Voting Rights Act, 24
VR, See virtual reality
Weinstein, Bernie, 25, 26
West Point, 26
West Point Fire House, 26
Westchester County, 26, 27, 29
William Steiger Occupational Safety and Health Act, 3

Willow Island, West Virginia, 4
Woolworth, 24
worker responsibility, 16
workers' compensation, 2, 7, 8
World Trade Center, 2, 3, 34
World War I, 20
World War II, 20, 22
World's Fair, 23-25
Xerox, 27
Xi Jinping, President, 81
Zhagnay v. Royal Realty, 12
Zorich, Paul S., 21

www.ingramcontent.com/pod-product-compliance
Lightning Source LLC
Chambersburg PA
CBHW060839190426
43197CB00040B/2703